How Things Work

The Nature Company Discoveries Library published by Time-Life Books

Conceived and produced by
Weldon Owen Pty Limited
43 Victoria Street, McMahons Point,
NSW, 2060, Australia
A member of the
Weldon Owen Group of Companies
Sydney • San Francisco
Copyright © 1996 US Weldon Owen Inc.
Copyright © 1996 Weldon Owen Pty Limited
Reprinted 1997

THE NATURE COMPANY
Priscilla Wrubel, Ed Strobin, Steve Manning,
Georganne Papac, Tracy Fortini

TIME-LIFE BOOKS
Time-Life Books is a division of Time Life Inc.
Time-Life is a trademark of Time Warner Inc.
U.S.A.

Time-Life Custom Publishing
Vice President and Publisher: Terry Newell
Director of New Product Development:
Quentin McAndrew
Managing Editor: Donia Ann Steele
Director of Sales: Neil Levin
Director of Financial Operations: J. Brian Birky

WELDON OWEN Pty Limited
Chairman: Kevin Weldon
President: John Owen
Publisher: Sheena Coupe
Managing Editor: Rosemary McDonald
Project Editors: Jean Coppendale,
Selena Quintrell Hand
Text Editors: Claire Craig, Gillian Gillett
Art Director: Sue Burk
Designer: Kylie Mulquin
Assistant Designers: Regina Safro, Melissa Wilton
Visual Research Coordinator: Jenny Mills
Visual Research: Kristina Sturm
Production Manager: Caroline Webber
Production Assistant: Kylie Lawson
Vice President, International Sales:
Stuart Laurence
Coeditions Director: Derek Barton

Text: Ian Graham

Illustrators: Colin Brown/Garden
Studio; Lynette R. Cook; Christer
Eriksson; Rod Ferring; Chris
Lyon/Brihton Illustration; Martin
Macrae/Folio; David Mathews/
Brihton Illustration; Peter Mennim;
Darren Pattenden/Garden Studio;
Oliver Rennert; Trevor Ruth;
Stephen Seymour /Bernard
Thornton Artists, UK;
Nick Shewring/Garden
Studio; Kevin Stead; Ross
Watton/Garden Studio;
Rod Westblade;
David Wood

Library of Congress
Cataloging-in-
Publication Data
Graham, Ian, 1953-
How things work / Ian Graham.
      p. cm. -- (Discoveries Library)
   Includes index.
   ISBN 0-8094-9249-0

   1. Technology--Miscellanea--Juvenile
literature. [1. Technology--Miscellanea.]
I. Title. II. Series.
T48.G68 1996
600--dc20   95-32819

Manufactured by Mandarin Offset
Printed in China

A Weldon Owen Production

How Things Work

CONSULTING EDITORS

Alison Porter
Education Unit Manager
The National Museum of Science and Industry, London

Eryl Davies
Media Consultant
Science and Technology, London

TIME
LIFE
BOOKS

Contents

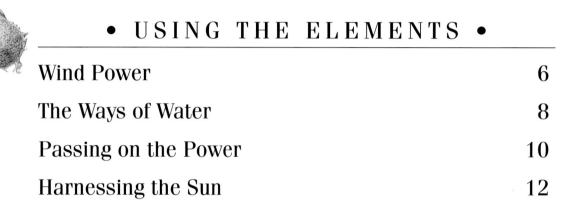

Wind Power

People have used the power of the wind for more than 5,000 years. It propelled their sailing boats over rivers, lakes and oceans; it turned the heavy blades of windmills to grind grain and pump water. Wind has energy because it is always moving in one direction or another. This energy can be caught, or harnessed, by large sails or blades. When electricity was developed in the nineteenth century, wind power did not seem as efficient as this marvelous new source of power, and most windmills disappeared. But wind power is making a comeback. Today, modern versions of windmills called wind turbines are used to generate electricity. Groups of wind turbines with long, thin metal or plastic blades, which look like airplane propellers on top of tall thin towers, are often erected together in wind farms that stretch across the landscape. By the middle of the twenty-first century, one-tenth of the world's electricity could be powered by wind turbines.

WIND FARMS
These are built in very windy areas and are controlled by computers that turn their blades into the wind. When the wind turns the blades, the spinning motion is converted into electricity.

Blades
The blades of the turbine are set at an angle that can be changed to suit the wind's speed or direction.

WIND-ASSISTED TANKER
This ship has stiff fiberglass sails as well as engines. It can save fuel by using sails whenever there is enough wind. Computers calculate the wind speed and indicate when it is time to unfold the sails.

Cables
Underground cables collect the electricity produced by the turbines at a wind farm.

Gearbox
The gearbox, driven by the turbine shaft, controls the speed of the generator.

Generator
The generator converts the spinning motion into electricity.

Turbine shaft
Wind turns the blades, which turn the central turbine shaft. The speed of the shaft varies according to the strength of the wind.

Nacelle
The nacelle (the part that contains the machinery) pivots to keep the blades pointing into the wind. The angle of the blades is set automatically to suit the wind speed.

Tower
The tower holds the blades at a safe height above the ground and contains the cables that carry the electricity underground.

Canvas-covered sails
Canvas sheeting stretched over the wooden frame of the sails caught the wind and moved the sails around.

MAKE YOUR OWN WINDMILL

Cut one-third of the way across a square of paper from each corner, and make a small hole in each corner (Step 1). Pull the four corners into the middle of the sheet (Step 2). Fasten by pushing a tack or drawing pin through the middle. Attach to a drinking straw at the back, making sure your windmill can spin freely (Step 3). Now blow on it or hold it in the breeze.

Step 1

Step 2

Step 3

TIMES PAST
This kind of windmill was used many years ago to grind grain.

Cap
The cap carrying the sails could turn so that the sails faced into the wind.

Fantail
Wind blowing against the fantail made it spin and turned the mill cap until the sails faced the wind.

Grain hopper
Grain fell from a container, called a hopper, down to the two grindstones below.

Driveshaft
This used the turning motion of the sails to move the grindstones.

Grindstones
Two heavy stones rotated and crushed the grain beneath them.

Discover more in Riding on Air

The Ways of Water

Water covers more than two-thirds of the Earth's surface and is constantly on the move. It rushes along rivers and streams; it flows into oceans. This endless movement of water creates energy that can be harnessed. For centuries, people have channeled flowing water into waterwheels that turn to grind grain. Hydroelectric power stations use water in a similar way, but to generate electricity. These enormous concrete constructions are usually found in mountainous regions where there is a high rainfall. Engineers build huge dams across steep-sided valleys. Turbines (modern versions of ancient wooden waterwheels) are placed in the path of the water that gushes with force through the dam. This torrent of water strikes the angled blades of the turbines, which begin to spin and extract an incredible amount of energy from the water. The process of producing hydroelectric power is set in motion.

Transmission lines
Strengthened electric cables called transmission lines carry electricity away from the power plant.

Spillway
The spillway gates are opened to release water when the level of water behind the dam is too high.

Control room
The operation of the entire power plant is directed from the control room.

WATERING THE LAND
The water for this insectlike irrigation system is coming from the dam of a hydroelectric power station.

Drift tube
Water leaves the turbines through the drift tube.

Reservoir
The deep lake that forms behind the dam wall is called a reservoir. The reservoir is built to make sure there is always enough water to operate the generators.

Dam walls
These are usually curved to withstand the enormous force of water pressing against them. The walls are thicker at the base than the top.

Transformers
Transformers boost the electrical force from the generators to more than 200,000 volts.

Penstock
This channels water from the reservoir through the dam to the turbines.

Generators
The spinning turbines are connected by shafts to electricity generators. When the turbines spin, the generators make electricity.

Turbines
Water flowing through tunnels in the dam makes the turbines spin at high speed. Once the energy has been removed, the water flows away through the center of the turbines.

MAKE YOUR OWN WATERWHEEL

Cut four pieces of cardboard 1½ in x ¾ in (4 cm x 2 cm) and collect an empty thread spool and drinking straw (Step 1). Glue each piece of cardboard to the thread spool (Step 2) and push the drinking straw through the middle so that your waterwheel can spin easily. Hold the wheel under a running faucet. When water hits the card paddles, the wheel will turn (Step 3).

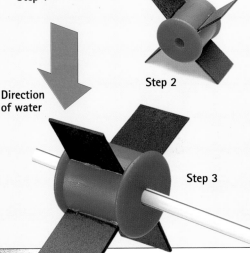

Step 1

Step 2

Direction of water

Step 3

A DAILY GRIND
This water-powered hammer is used in Laos in Southeast Asia to grind rice. When the paddles are turned by the flow of the river, the crossbeam at the end of the axle raises the hammer, then releases it to fall on the rice below.

Discover more in Roaming the Oceans

9

Passing on the Power

Electricity has to be sent from the power station where it is made to the homes and businesses where it is used. Whether the power station is nuclear powered, hydroelectric or burns coal, the electricity it makes is distributed in the same way. Transformers at the power station boost the electricity to a very high voltage—hundreds of thousands of volts. The electricity is then carried by metal cables suspended from tall transmission towers, or pylons. It usually ends its journey by passing along underground cables. By the time it reaches your home, transformers have reduced its voltage to a level that depends on which country you live in. Electricity generated in one place can be sent to another part of the country if more power is needed.

TURBOGENERATOR
Electricity is made by a turbogenerator—a generator driven by a turbine. When a wire moves near a magnet, electricity flows along the wire. Inside the generator, strong magnets make electricity flow through coils of wire.

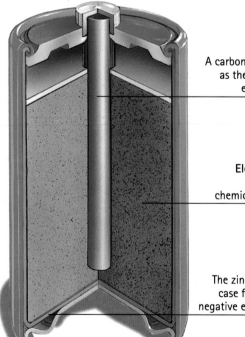

Anode
A carbon rod acts as the positive electrode.

Electrolyte
This is a chemical paste.

Cathode
The zinc battery case forms the negative electrode.

Rotor
The rotor consists of coils of wire that rotate at high speed. Electric current flowing through the coils creates powerful magnetic fields around them.

ELECTRICITY DISTRIBUTION
Electricity generated at a power station is distributed through a network of cables above and below the ground.

Transformers
Transformers increase the voltage before electricity is transmitted.

BATTERIES
When a battery is connected to an electric circuit, a chemical reaction between the negative terminal (cathode) and a liquid or paste (electrolyte) creates a current. This current travels round the circuit and returns to the battery at the positive electrode (anode).

10

A Bright Idea

Most light bulbs contain a thin coiled wire filament that heats up and glows when an electric current flows through it. They are called incandescent bulbs (left). An energy efficient bulb (right) is a fluorescent tube that needs less electricity to produce the same amount of light as a normal bulb. When an electric current passes through mercury vapor inside the tube, the vapor releases invisible ultraviolet rays, and the coating on the inside of the bulb converts them into visible light.

Stator
The stator, which does not move, is made from coils of wire surrounding the rotor. As the rotor turns, its magnetic fields cut through the stator coils and make an electric current flow through them.

Did You Know?

Power stations have to be ready to boost electricity production whenever demand suddenly increases. In many countries, television schedules help to predict power demands! At the end of films or major sporting events, the demand for electricity soars as millions of television viewers switch on their electric kettles to make tea or coffee.

Power take-off cables
Thick cables lead electric current away from the generator.

Transmission towers
The transmission lines are held high above the ground by tall transmission towers. Glass or ceramic insulators between the metal towers and the cables stop the current from running down the towers into the ground.

Transmission lines
Cables strengthened by steel carry the current.

Street transformer
Before electricity reaches your home, its voltage is reduced by transformers. The voltage level depends on the country you live in.

Home
Electricity enters your home through a meter that measures how much electricity is used.

11

SAVING ENERGY

An energy-efficient house is designed to minimize energy waste. It generates its own electricity, but it is still connected to the national power grid. If it generates more electricity than it needs, the excess is supplied to the grid. If it needs more electricity, this is supplied by the grid.

Keeping warm
Most of the heat lost by a house escapes through the roof. The roof of an energy-efficient house is lined with insulation material to stop heat from escaping.

Solar panels
When the sun shines on a solar panel, solar energy is converted into electricity to power electrical appliances in the house, such as water heaters or cooling fans.

• USING THE ELEMENTS •

Harnessing the Sun

The sun is an extraordinarily powerful form of energy. In fact, the Earth receives 20,000 times more energy from the sun than we currently use. If we used much more of this source of heat and light, it could supply all the power needed throughout the world. We can harness energy from the sun, called "solar" energy, in many ways. Satellites in space have large panels covered with solar cells that change sunlight directly into electrical power. Some buildings have solar collectors that use solar energy to heat water. These panels are covered with glass and are painted black inside to absorb as much heat as possible. Some experimental electric cars are even powered by solar panels. Solar energy is a clean fuel, but fossil fuels, such as oil or coal, release harmful substances into the air when they are burned. Fossil fuels will run out eventually, but solar energy will continue to reach the Earth long after the last coal has been mined and the last oil well has run dry.

The sunny side
The house is built with one long side facing the sun so that it can absorb as much solar energy as possible during the day.

Small windows
Windows that do not face the sun are smaller, to reduce heat loss.

Water tanks
Hot water from the roof-top solar collectors is stored in tanks for later use. The tanks are insulated to stop the heat from escaping.

SOLAR CELLS

Solar cells convert light directly into electricity. Light reaches the cell through a transparent protective coating. The first layer is made from a material called N-type silicon (silicon is one of the most plentiful elements in the Earth's crust). N-type silicon is specially treated so that it has more electrons than normal silicon. The second layer is made from P-type silicon. This has gaps in its structure because it has less electrons. Sunlight gives electrons enough energy to jump from the N-type silicon to the P-type to fill the gaps. When electrons move, they make an electric current. The tiny currents made by hundreds or thousands of solar cells are added together to make an electric current that is large enough to power equipment.

Solar cell

Sunlight

Protective coating

N-type silicon

P-type silicon

Large windows
Windows facing the sun are large so that plenty of solar energy can pass through and warm the rooms inside. In the evening, when the sun sets, heavy curtains or shutters are closed over the windows to stop the heat from escaping.

Walls
The walls are filled with insulating materials to stop heat from escaping through them.

Skylights
These let in natural light and can be opened to let warm air escape.

Cover up
Awnings shield windows from the excessive heat and glare of the sun.

WARMING UP

Greenhouses are made of glass and have slanted roofs to allow the maximum amount of sunlight to enter. The sun's heat is trapped inside, which raises the temperature inside the greenhouse and helps the plants to grow. Plants in a greenhouse can be grown all year around.

13

Did You Know?

People have made instruments to measure the passing of time for at least 3,000 years. The sundial was developed from a simple observation. As the Earth turns, the sun appears to cross the sky and the shadows it casts move across the ground. If the positions of the shadows are marked at regular intervals, they can be used to tell the time.

Escapement
This regulates the speed of the clock. It consists of an anchor that rocks from side to side, and an escape wheel that is repeatedly caught and released by the anchor.
Hour hand
The hour hand makes one revolution every 12 hours.
Minute hand
The minute hand moves 12 times faster than the hour hand and makes one revolution every hour.
Pendulum
The swinging pendulum regulates the rocking motion of the anchor.

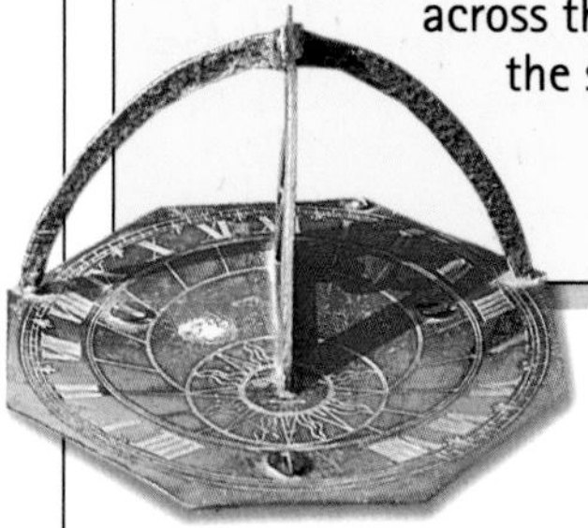

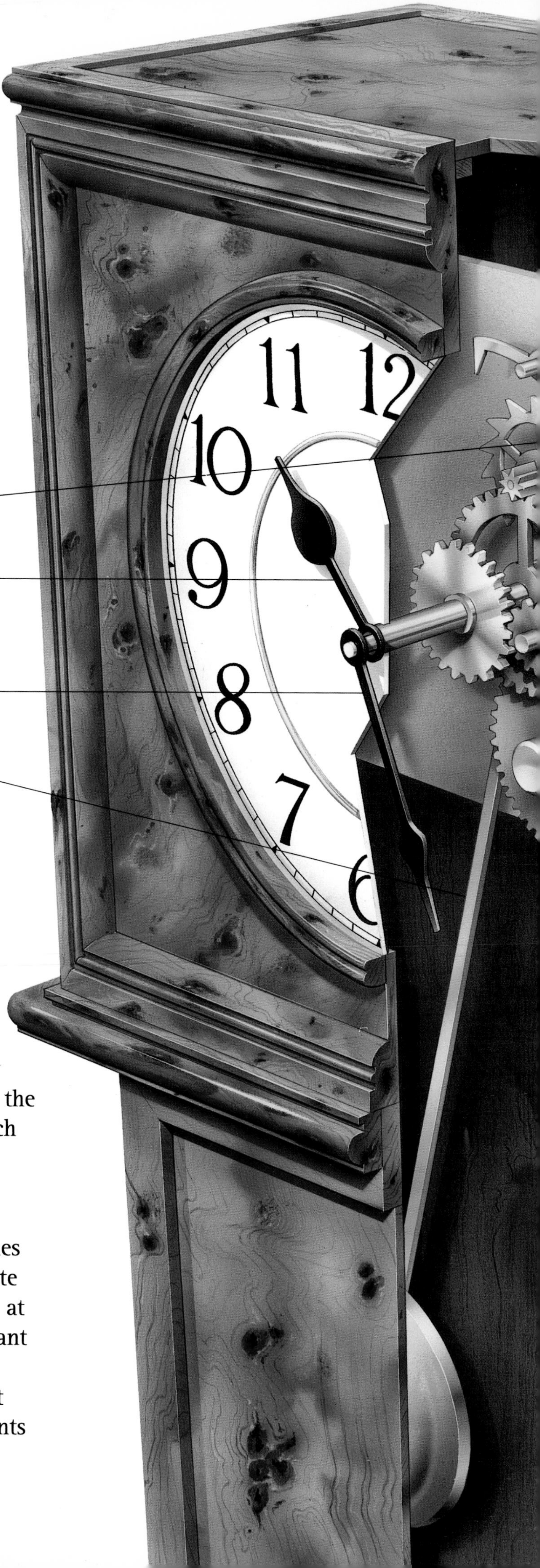

• MACHINES •

About Time

People have been keeping the time for thousands of years. The first time-keeping devices were very inaccurate. They measured time by the sun, or by the falling levels of water or sand. Mechanical clocks are much more accurate. They have three main parts: an energy supply, a mechanism for regulating the energy and a way of showing the passing of time. The energy is supplied by a coiled spring or a weight. The spring unwinds, or the weight falls, and turns a series of interlocking, toothed wheels. Hands linked to the wheels rotate around a dial. For the clock to be accurate, the hands must turn at a constant speed. In large clocks, a pendulum swings at a constant rate and regulates the movement of the escapement. Digital or electronic watches have a piece of quartz crystal that vibrates at 32,768 times a second. An electronic circuit uses these movements to turn the hands or change numbers on the watch face.

ON YOUR MARK, GET SET, GO!
Athletes often cross the finish line at exactly the same moment and it is difficult to decide who has won the race. Officials accurately record the athletes' race times so that very close finishes can be separated by degrees of a second.

Gears
These make sure that the minute hand goes around 12 times faster than the hour hand.

Weight
This hangs on a cord wound around a shaft so that the weight turns the shaft to move the gears.

KEEPING TIME
Athletes train hard for their events. Stopwatches can help them monitor their progress by measuring times to within 100th of a second. Some stopwatches can also store up to 100 laps in their memories and even print times using built-in printers.

THINGS IN COMMON

Pendulum clocks and digital watches are very different in size, but they are made from the same basic building blocks. Both have an oscillator that moves or swings at a regular rate (left), a device that turns these movements into time-keeping pulses (center) and a display for showing the time (right).

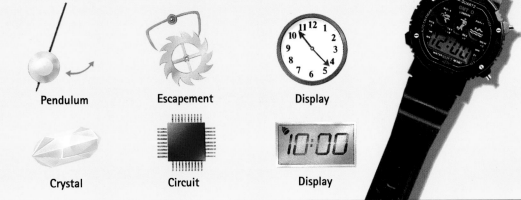

Pendulum

Escapement

Display

Crystal

Circuit

Display

Discover more in Computer Friendly

VACUUM CLEANER

A vacuum cleaner works in a similar way to a straw. When you drink through a straw you suck out the air and this draws up the fluid. A vacuum cleaner creates a powerful flow of air that sucks up dust and dirt through a hose and traps it inside the machine.

FAST FOOD

A microwave oven uses powerful radio waves of a very short wavelength (microwaves) to cook food very quickly. These waves heat the inside as well as the outside of food immediately. In more traditional ovens, the heat takes longer to cook the inside of the food.

• MACHINES •

Saving Time and Effort

We use machines around the house every day. They make our lives easier and give us time to do other things. Hundreds of years ago, for example, household chores took most of the day. Water was carted from a well, food was cooked over an open fire, and houses were swept with branches. Today, most homes have labor-saving devices, which are designed to make jobs around the home less of an effort. Washing machines automatically wash and rinse clothes, then spin them to force out most of the water. Some even dry the clothes completely. Refrigerators and freezers keep food fresh longer so that we do not need to shop every day. Dishwashers, remote controls for televisions and videos, microwave ovens and vacuum cleaners are some of the appliances found in many homes throughout the world.

Dust bag
Air carries dust and dirt into the dust bag. The air then escapes through tiny holes in the bag and leaves the dust trapped inside. Some vacuum cleaners have a "micro-filter," with even smaller holes in it, to trap the tiniest dust particles.

Fan
A spinning fan sucks air and dust through the flexible hose into the vacuum cleaner.

Motor
The fan is driven by an electric motor. Some vacuum cleaners can vary the speed of the motor so that the suction power can be adjusted to clean different surfaces.

Insulation
The oven is double-walled and insulated. This stops heat from leaking out of the oven.

Magnetron
Microwaves are produced by a device called a magnetron.

Waveguide
The waveguide is a hollow tube that channels microwaves from the magnetron into the oven.

HEATING BY MICROWAVES

Water is made up of particles called water molecules. When water molecules are struck by microwaves, they vibrate very quickly. When molecules of any substance vibrate quickly, the substance heats up. Most food contains water, so when food is placed in a microwave oven, the microwaves cook it quickly by heating the water inside it.

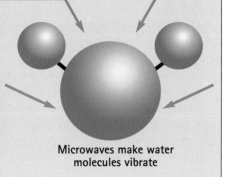

Microwaves

Microwaves make water molecules vibrate

0:58

FLUSHING TOILET
Pressing a button on top of a toilet causes water to rush out of the cistern. The float in the cistern falls and opens a water valve to refill the cistern. As the water level rises, so does the float, closing the valve so that the cistern does not overflow.

Valve

Float

Cistern

Control panel
The cooking time and the oven heat are set by using the control panel.

Mesh screen
The food can be seen through the mesh screen on the see-through door, but the microwaves cannot escape from the oven.

Walls
The walls of the oven reflect the microwaves onto the food.

Turntable
The turntable rotates so that food cooks evenly.

Discover more in Keeping in Touch

Office Essentials

Modern businesses depend on being able to send and receive information quickly. Telephones enable people to talk to each other over long distances, but the worldwide telephone network carries much more than people's voices. Computers and fax machines, for example, use this network to send information to each other. "Fax" is short for "facsimile transmission" (facsimile means copy). A fax machine can transmit a copy of an image on paper—a printed document, handwritten message or drawing—to anywhere in the world within seconds. It does this by changing the information on the paper into electrical signals, then converting these into sounds that are sent along normal telephone lines. Another fax machine receives the sounds and changes them back into a printed copy of the original image. Computers exchange information by telephone in the same way. Some of the information exchanged by computers is called electronic mail or E-mail, because it is an electronic version of the ordinary postal system.

Drum
The rotating drum attracts black toner powder onto itself, then transfers the powder onto the paper. This creates an image on the page.

Print head
A row of lights flashes on and off as the charged drum rotates next to it. The electric charge on the drum is weakened wherever light strikes it. Black toner powder sticks only to the uncharged parts of the drum and forms an image of the transmitted document on it.

Numerical keypad
Telephone numbers are dialed by using this pad.

One-touch keys
Frequently used telephone numbers are keyed into the fax machine and stored in an electronic memory. When a number is selected from the memory, by pressing one of these buttons, the machine dials it automatically.

Image sensor
The electrical signal produced by the photosensor is changed into sounds that are transmitted down a telephone line.

FAXING A MESSAGE

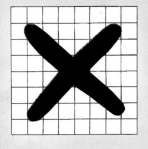

The fax machine divides the image on the paper into a grid of tiny squares and detects whether each square is light or dark.

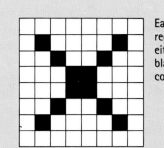

Each square is registered as either completely black or completely white.

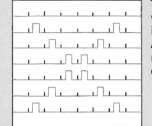

The pattern of black and white squares is changed into an electrical signal. A pulse of electricity represents a dark square.

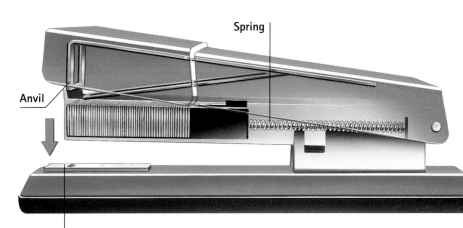

Spring

Anvil

Plate

STAPLING TOGETHER

A stapler fastens sheets of paper together with short lengths of wire called staples. The staples are glued in a row, but when the stapler's jaws are pressed down over the paper, one staple is separated from the rest and forced through the paper.
A metal plate with specially shaped grooves in the base bends the ends of the staple inward so that it cannot fall out again.

STICK-ON NOTES

Stick-on notes can be stuck to almost any surface, peeled off again easily and stuck somewhere else. The secret lies in the gum on the back. It is not as sticky as the gum on adhesive tape, and the notes can be peeled off paper without damaging it.

Fuser unit
The paper leaves the machine through the fuser unit, a pair of rollers that melts the toner powder and fuses it to the paper by heat and pressure.

Transfer unit
The transfer unit charges the paper so that it attracts toner powder off the drum and onto the paper.

Paper
A plain paper fax machine prints copies of documents onto sheets of paper that are stored in a tray at the bottom of the machine.

This simple electrical signal is changed into a complex code. As documents are usually printed on white paper, white is given a shorter code than black. The code is changed into sounds that can be sent down a telephone line.

The receiving fax machine changes the sounds into an electrical signal, which controls a printer.

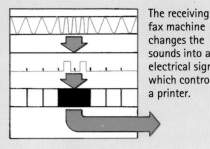

By printing line after line of black spots, the receiving fax machine builds up a copy of the original document.

19

Jib
The cross arm, or jib, suspends the hook that lifts the load. The jib is suspended by cables or steel rods from the top of the tower.

Counterweight
Concrete slabs on one side of the tower balance the weight of the loads it lifts on the other side.

Operator's cab
The crane operator sits in a cab at the top of the tower and moves the load by operating controls. The front of the cab is made from glass to give the operator a clear view of the hook, from the ground up.

• MACHINES •

Building Upward

Machines are used in the construction industry to lift, move, cut, drill and connect the various materials used. A tower crane, for example, is used to lift heavy materials up to the workers. The horizontal arm of the tower crane is called the jib. This can swing around horizontally, but it cannot be raised or lowered. The crane's hook is raised and lowered by winding the cable it hangs from around a large motorized drum. Thousands of tons of materials have to be delivered to the construction site. One of these materials, concrete, is delivered by concrete mixers. Their drums rotate constantly to stop the concrete inside from setting hard before it is poured out wherever it is needed. Pulleys (wheels with grooves around their rims) are often used on building sites to help move very heavy loads. When a rope or chain is threaded around several pulleys, a pull on the rope or chain is enhanced, or magnified, by the pulleys to enable a small effort to move a heavy load.

Trolley
The hook is suspended from a trolley that can be moved by cables to any point along the jib.

Pulleys
Pulleys allow the crane to lift very heavy loads.

MAKE YOUR OWN BLOCK AND TACKLE

A number of pulleys used together is called a block and tackle. You can make your own block and tackle by threading a length of string through the hole in the middle of two thread spools (Step 1) and tying the ends to a hook. Thread a second length of string through the hole in the middle of two more thread spools (Step 2) and tie the ends of the string to the handle of a bucket. Tie a third length of string to the hook (Step 3) and thread it around the spools as shown. The top thread spools are the block and the lower spools are the tackle. Pulling the string lifts the bucket. Adding more pulleys makes the load even easier to raise. Try making a block and tackle from six pulleys to see the difference.

Step 1

Step 2

Step 3

Winch motor
Cables driven by the winch motor move the hook and trolley.

GOING UP
A tower crane is built at the construction site and grows with the building. Each new section is slotted into a frame fitted over the tower. This frame is then raised to leave a space for the next new section.

Tower
The tower is built from a steel frame of triangles because the triangle is a very strong shape. An open frame is used instead of a solid tower because it weighs less and allows the wind to blow through it, not push against it.

ALL MIXED UP
When the drum of a concrete mixer turns, curved blades inside mix the concrete. When the drum turns in the opposite direction, the blades work like an Archimedes' screw: they force the concrete out of the drum until it tumbles down a chute onto the ground.

Making Shopping Easy

Technology has made shopping quick and convenient. Automated teller machines (ATMs) give us immediate access to our money and reduce the need to stand in long lines inside the bank. Personal identification numbers (PINs) and cash cards replace passbooks and withdrawal slips. All cash cards have a magnetic strip on their backs. When the code and information stored here match the information in the bank's computer, the machine gives you the requested amount of money. Computers and lasers speed up the service at checkout counters in stores. A laser scans the barcode of every product and tells the computerized cash register how much the product costs. It also records how many of a certain product have sold, so that more stock can be ordered when necessary. Some products have security tags attached to them. If anyone tries to take a tagged product out of the store, sensors at the door detect the tag and sound an alarm.

PRICE SCAN

As the laser beam scans the barcode, a light-sensitive sensor in the handset picks up its reflections. An electric current flows through the sensor and produces electrical pulses in a pattern that matches the barcode's pattern of black lines. A pair of thin lines in the middle divides the barcode in two. The first half of the code contains the manufacturer's name and the second half is the code for the product. The pairs of thin lines at each end of the pattern tell the computer where the code starts and finishes. A barcode computer can always "translate" the code lines because the same standard—the Universal Product Code—is used for barcodes all over the world.

DID YOU KNOW?

The printing on paper currency can be copied by forgers. In 1988, the Commonwealth Reserve Bank of Australia issued a plastic folding banknote that is very difficult to copy.

Currency cassettes
Banknotes are stored in boxes called cassettes.

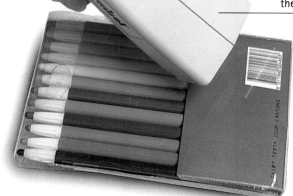

Barcode scanner
A laser in the handset scans the barcode. The sensor identifies the product and its price, then sends these details to the cash register.

BANKING MADE EASY

An automated teller machine (ATM) enables people to withdraw money from an account. Most ATMs can also show us how much money is in our account and can transfer money from one account to another.

Card reader
The card is drawn inside the machine by motorized rollers. Information recorded invisibly on a magnetic strip on its back is read in a way that is similar to a tape being played in a tape recorder.

Screen
The screen gives step-by-step instructions for using the machine.

Printer
The printer prints out a record of the cash withdrawal, and the ATM pushes out a receipt for the customer.

Keypad
The card-owner enters his or her unique personal identification number (PIN) into the machine by pressing keys on the pad.

Currency dispenser
Banknotes from the currency cassettes are counted and issued by the currency dispenser. They are pushed out of the machine through a pair of motorized rollers.

Computer processor
All the operations within the machine and all the messages that appear on its screen are controlled by a computer processor.

SECURITY TAGS

Plastic security tags contain coils of wire that can be detected magnetically or by radio waves when they pass through the sensors at the store entrance.

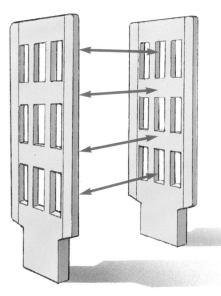

Paying by Credit Card

When a payment is made by credit card, the salesperson slides the card through a card reader. It reads information recorded on the card's magnetic strip and sends it by telephone to a central computer. This checks the details and approves the payment. Later, the card's owner receives a bill for this payment. Payments are also made in this way with debit cards, but the amounts are transferred from the card-owner's bank to the store.

Discover more in Recording Sound

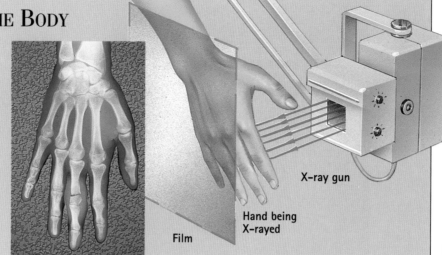

PICTURING THE BODY

The chance discovery of X-rays by Wilhelm Konrad Roentgen in 1895 was a medical breakthrough. X-rays pass through soft parts of the body and darken a photographic film on the other side. Dense parts, such as bones and teeth, block the rays so that a clear "shadow" is made on the film.

Processed film image

X-ray gun

Hand being X-rayed

Film

• MACHINES •

At the Hospital

In hospitals, medical staff use machines and instruments to help people. Ultrasound scanners, X-ray machines and other medical equipment can be used to diagnose an illness, treat an injury or monitor changes in the patient's condition. More complex scanners use the high-speed processing power of computers to create intricate pictures. These scanners can show cross-sections of a body, three-dimensional views of internal organs, and pictures of the brain showing which parts of it are active while the patient is thinking, seeing, hearing or moving. These pictures can be seen on the scanner's own special screen, and can also be printed out on paper or on film. Such a detailed view of a disease or an injury allows doctors to see all the angles of a medical problem and then figure out the best way to treat it.

Hand-held probe

Diaphragm

Earpiece

LISTENING IN
A stethoscope detects and amplifies sounds from inside the body and passes them through tubes to earpieces in the doctor's ears. The circular head of the instrument (above) has two devices for picking up sound: a diaphragm on one side that picks up high-pitched sounds, and a bell on the other side (the underside in this picture) for low-pitched sounds.

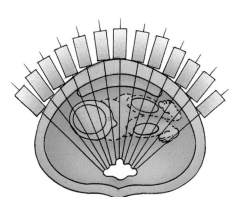

AN INSIDE VIEW
This woman is having an ultrasound examination of her baby. The probe that is held on her stomach sends bursts of ultrasound down into her body. It also receives the reflections bouncing back again. Reflections from deeper inside the patient take longer to bounce back. The machine records the different "flight times" of the sound waves and produces a picture of a part of the body. Unborn babies are often examined in this way.

Scanning
The ultrasound probe is moved from side to side, sending ultrasonic vibrations down into the patient's body. When the ultrasound vibrations strike anything inside the body, some are reflected. Others pass through to be reflected by deeper layers.

Generating an image
The ultrasound reflections are received by the probe and combined by a computer to make a picture of the patient's internal organs. If the patient is a pregnant woman, an ultrasound scan shows a picture of her unborn baby and its internal organs.

Inside information
An ultrasound operator can tell from the picture on the machine's screen whether an unborn baby is a boy or a girl. He or she can also examine the baby's internal organs, especially the heart, to make sure that the fetus is developing normally. Ultrasound can also confirm the number of babies the mother is carrying.

DID YOU KNOW?
In the 1950s, doctors realized that an unborn baby in its mother's fluid-filled womb was like a submarine in the sea. Submarines use a system called sonar (from SOund Navigation And Ranging) to detect objects near them. Sonar sends out bursts of ultrasound and detects reflections that bounce back from solid objects. This system was adapted and used to examine people in hospitals.

Keeping in Touch

Radio waves are vibrating, invisible waves of energy. They are similar to light waves, and are very useful for carrying information across great distances. Radio and television programs, for example, travel from transmitters all over the world to our homes. As radio waves can travel through outer space, astronauts' voices and information collected by satellites can also be transmitted by radio. Many natural objects in the universe send out radio signals that radio telescopes on Earth can receive. Whatever a radio receiver is used for, it always has the same parts. An aerial, or receiving antenna, picks up the radio signals and feeds them down a cable to the receiver. A tuner selects particular signals and discards all the rest, and an amplifier strengthens the selected signals. A radio telescope receives data, which can be displayed as perhaps pictures or charts; while a radio at home changes the radio signals it receives into sound.

RADIO TELESCOPE

A radio telescope forms images of the sky from very faint radio signals. They are so weak that they cannot be used until a series of amplifiers makes them 1,000 million million times larger. The telescope scans an object in the sky from side to side and builds up a picture of it from a series of horizontal lines.

Metal dish

Receiving antenna

Radio signals

LISTENING IN

A radio telescope picks up radio signals from the rest of the universe by bouncing them off a broad metal dish so that they come together at a single point where a receiving antenna is located.

Control room

DID YOU KNOW?

The world's largest radio telescope is in Arecibo, Puerto Rico. It was built by lining a natural hollow in the ground with wire mesh to form a reflecting dish 1,000 ft (305 m) across. The Arecibo telescope cannot be moved, but most radio telescopes can be tilted and turned to point at any part of the sky.

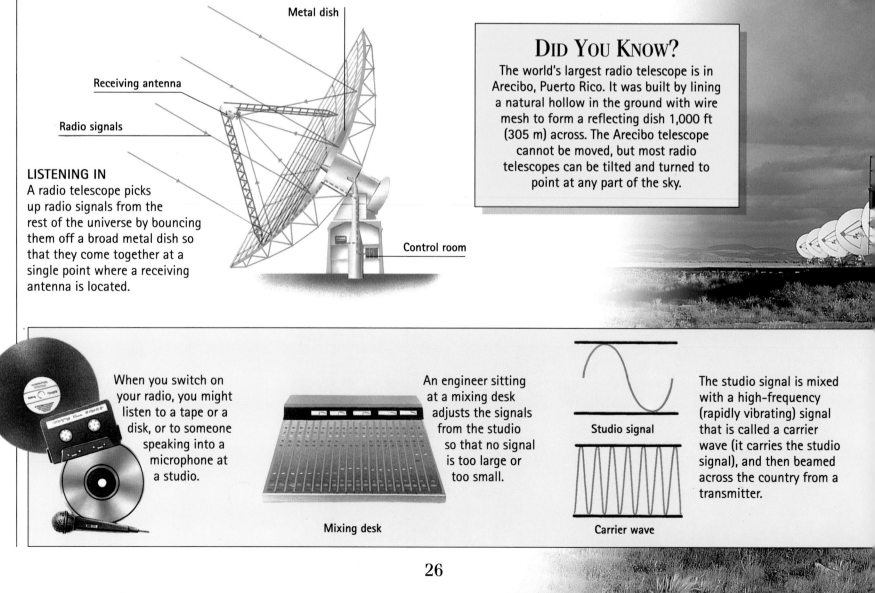

When you switch on your radio, you might listen to a tape or a disk, or to someone speaking into a microphone at a studio.

An engineer sitting at a mixing desk adjusts the signals from the studio so that no signal is too large or too small.

Mixing desk

Studio signal

Carrier wave

The studio signal is mixed with a high-frequency (rapidly vibrating) signal that is called a carrier wave (it carries the studio signal), and then beamed across the country from a transmitter.

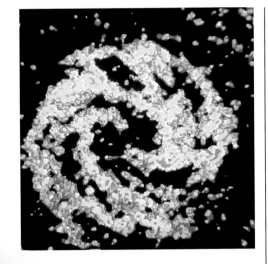

THE RADIO SKY
Pictures made by radio telescopes are not like normal pictures of the sky. Radio waves have no color, so the colors in a radio telescope picture are added by computer.

Frequency modulation (FM)

Amplitude modulation (AM)

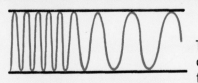

The studio signal changes either the frequency (speed of vibration) of the carrier wave, which is called frequency modulation; or the carrier wave's amplitude (size), which is called amplitude modulation.

Various signals flow around a radio antenna and create tiny electrical currents. The radio is tuned into just one of these signals, which is separated from its carrier wave. The signal is then amplified (made more powerful) by the radio, and the speaker changes it back into sound. ⌃

Antenna

Tuner

Speaker

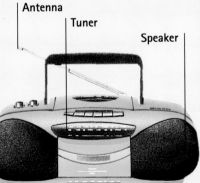

Messages from Space

In the sky
A low-flying satellite orbits at a height of about 155–186 miles (250-300 km) just outside most of the Earth's atmosphere. It can dip down to as low as 74 miles (120 km) to take close-up photographs of interesting places. Its advanced camera systems can see details as small as 2 in (5 cm) across.

Satellites circling the Earth send us pictures of the weather and relay telephone calls and television programs around the world. They also study vast areas of the Earth and its oceans, taking photographs and measurements with their cameras and instruments and beaming them down to Earth by radio. Some satellites circle the planet from pole to pole; others circle around the equator. Most satellites orbit the Earth at a height of between 124 miles (200 km) and 496 miles (800 km) and have to travel at a speed of 5 miles (8 km) per second to stay in orbit. Communications and weather satellites are boosted to a height of 22,320 miles (36,000 km)—much higher than other satellites. At this height above the equator, a satellite circles the Earth once every 24 hours, the same time the Earth takes to spin once on its axis. This kind of orbit is called "geostationary" because the satellite seems to hover over the same spot on Earth. It takes three satellites in geostationary orbit to relay telephone calls between any two points on Earth.

Communications satellite
A communications satellite, or comsat, works a little like a mirror in the sky. It receives radio signals beamed up to it from Earth, amplifies them and sends them back to a different place on Earth.

A LIVE BROADCAST
Satellites enable events such as the Olympic Games to be watched anywhere in the world seconds after they happen.

Gas tanks
The satellite uses jets of gas from its gas tanks to stop it from drifting out of position.

Communications circuits
The satellite's communications circuits can relay tens of thousands of telephone calls at the same time.

28

PICTURING THE WEATHER

Satellite pictures can help a weather forecaster see how weather systems, such as cyclones, grow and move across the oceans. Views such as this would be impossible to obtain from the ground.

Weather satellite
The world's weather constantly changes, and the temperatures of the sea, the land and the clouds vary all the time. A weather satellite carries heat-sensitive cameras that continually monitor the weather.

STAYING IN ORBIT

If you could throw a ball hard enough, it would fly all the way around the Earth, because the curve of its fall would exactly match the curve of the Earth's surface. To see this in action, make two plastic balls— one 2 in (5 cm) across to represent gravity, and one ¾ in (2 cm) across to represent a satellite. Thread 20 in (51 cm) of string through a thread spool (Earth), and tie each end to a key. Push each key into one of the balls. Hold the thread spool and the large ball and start the small ball spinning. Let the large ball go. The satellite tries to fly away from Earth but gravity pulls it back. When the two forces are balanced, the satellite orbits Earth.

Solar panels
Solar panels change sunlight into electricity to supply power for the satellite's radio equipment.

Discover more in Reaching into Space

29

TELEPHONE

A telephone converts the sound of a caller's voice into an electric current and changes electric currents received from other telephones into sound.

Coil
An electrical signal received by the earpiece passes through a coil and creates a weak magnetic field around it.

Magnet
The magnet attracts or repels the coil and makes it vibrate.

Diaphragm
The diaphragm then vibrates to create a sound.

Diaphragm
The mouthpiece works in the opposite way to the earpiece. The caller's voice makes the diaphragm vibrate.

Coil
A coil of wire fixed to the diaphragm vibrates next to a magnet. The vibrations create an electric current that is sent on.

Shrinking the World

Distances are usually measured in miles or kilometers, but they can also be measured in time—the time it takes to communicate over a certain distance. In past centuries, the distance to the next town might have been measured by the time it took to travel there on foot or on horseback. A more distant town might be a week away and another continent might be several months away by ship. With telephones we can now communicate with someone thousands of miles away just as quickly as we can with someone in the next room. The size of the world seems to have shrunk. Electrical communication works by changing information into electrical signals that can be sent along cables. The first telephone calls made their entire journey as electrical signals in metal cables. Today, telephone calls can also travel in the form of infrared beams along fiber-optic cables or as radio waves relayed by satellites in space.

THE PATH OF A TELEPHONE CALL

Telephones are connected to a network of exchanges that are linked together by copper cables, fiber-optic cables or radio. Every telephone is identified by a unique number and the path a telephone call takes depends on the number that is dialed. Most telephones stay in one place and are connected to the nearest exchange by cable, but some are portable. Mobile telephones can be carried anywhere, even to another country. Every few minutes, they send out coded radio signals that identify them and let the network know where they are. This enables calls to be transmitted to the correct mobile telephone from the nearest radio antenna.

STRANGE BUT TRUE

The fiber optics that carry telephone calls are made of highly refined glass. A 12-mile (19-km) block of it would be as clear to see through as an ordinary window pane. A few fibers, enough to carry 100,000 telephone calls at the same time, can pass through the eye of a needle.

FIBER-OPTIC CABLES

In many parts of the world, metal telephone cables are being replaced by fiber-optic cables made of glass. Telephone calls travel along these cables as flickering infrared beams. Fiber-optic cables are much thinner, yet carry more calls than metal cables.

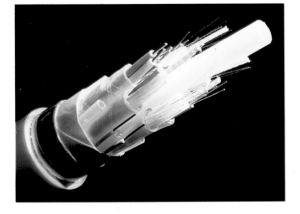

Antenna
The antenna detects radio waves for the telephone's radio receiver, and also sends them out from its transmitter.

Battery
A mobile telephone is powered by a battery. When the battery runs out of energy, it can be recharged (filled with more electrical energy) by a charging unit.

Keypad
Telephone numbers are dialed by pressing these keys.

Microphone
The microphone changes the speaker's voice into electrical signals.

MOBILE PHONE

Mobile telephones are linked to the international telephone network by radio. Every mobile telephone contains its own radio receiver and transmitter.

Earpiece
The earpiece changes electrical signals from the radio receiver into sound.

Display
A liquid crystal display shows the number being dialed.

1. Local exchange
A telephone call is sent through the caller's local exchange to the nearest main exchange by cable.

2. Main exchange
The main exchange sends the call on its way to the next main exchange via cables, optical fibers or radio signals.

3. Mobile network
Calls made to a mobile telephone are sent through the mobile telephone network.

4. Cell base station
The call is then sent to the mobile telephone from a nearby radio antenna.

Computer Friendly

Computers have become part of our everyday lives. We use them to store a vast amount of information and process it very quickly. The processing and storage are carried out by microscopic electronic circuits called chips. The master chip, the microprocessor, controls the computer. A microprocessor may contain several hundred thousand electronic components in a space that is no bigger than your thumbnail. The chips and the rest of the equipment form only one part of a computer, the hardware, but the computer also needs instructions to tell the hardware what to do. These instructions are called computer programs, or software. Software can make a computer perform a huge range of different jobs. It may turn the computer into a word processor for writing and storing documents, a games machine for having fun, an educational tool or a very fast calculating machine.

PERSONAL COMPUTER
Every computer, whatever its size and complexity, contains four basic elements: the input device, usually a keyboard; the memory, where information is stored; the central processing unit (CPU), which carries out the instructions; and the output device, usually a monitor and printer.

Monitor
A computer monitor looks like a small television screen. It receives and displays information from the computer.

Ball | **Wheel**

Buttons
A mouse may have one, two or three buttons.

CD-ROM drive
A CD-ROM (Compact Disk Read-Only Memory) can hold all sorts of information that can be copied from the CD-ROM onto the computer, but new information cannot be recorded on it.

DRIVING THE MOUSE
A mouse is used to steer a pointer around the screen. When you move the mouse, a ball underneath it rolls and makes two slotted wheels turn. As each wheel turns, a light shines through the slots and the flashes are detected by a sensor. The number and speed of the flashes show how far, how fast and in which direction the mouse is moving. When you "click" the button or buttons on the mouse, you select different options on the screen.

FLOPPY DISK DRIVE

The disk drive works like a tape recorder, but instead of recording information on magnetic tape it uses magnetic disks. With a disk slotted into the drive, which is positioned at the front of the computer, information can be copied onto the disk or from the disk onto the computer.

Read–write head
The read-write head records information onto the disk and reads it again when it is needed.

Case
A stiff plastic case protects the delicate disk.

DISK
Information is stored as magnetic patterns on a paper-thin disk.

Microprocessor
The microprocessor is a personal computer's master control chip. It contains the computer's central processing unit.

Speakers
A computer often has speakers to play music, sound effects or speech.

Keyboard
This is used to put information onto the computer.

DID YOU KNOW?

The idea of the computer dates back to the 1830s when English mathematician Charles Babbage tried to build a calculating machine called the Analytical Engine. Babbage failed because the parts for his machine could not be made with enough precision. However, many of his ideas were used more than 100 years later when the first computers were built.

Discover more in Recording Sound

33

Seeing clearly
The image is seen by looking into the eyepiece. It contains one or more lenses.

MICROSCOPE

The simplest microscope is a magnifying glass. However, a single lens can only magnify an object up to 15 times. For greater magnifications, a compound microscope with several lenses is used.

Objective lenses
Three or more objective lenses with a range of magnifying powers are fitted to a microscope. Each can be rotated to focus on the specimen.

Specimen
The specimen is placed between two pieces of glass, which must be thin enough for light to pass through them.

View of a butterfly wing with the naked eye

15 x magnified view of a butterfly wing

50 x magnified view of a butterfly wing

Light source
Light is reflected up to the specimen using an angled mirror.

A Closer Look

The human eye is an amazing organ, but there are many things it cannot see because they are too small or too far away. We use instruments to magnify tiny details so they are big enough for us to see. Microscopes, for example, can make small objects look 2,500 times bigger than they really are. Telescopes and binoculars produce magnified images of objects that appear too small to see clearly because they are so far away. These instruments are built with lenses, because lenses can bend light rays and make our eyes think that the light has come from a much larger object. Light enters the instruments through a type of lens called an objective lens. This forms an enlarged image of the object. We look at this image through another lens, the eyepiece, which magnifies it a little more.

Focusing knob
The object can be brought into sharp focus by turning the focusing knob. This moves the eyepieces closer to or farther away from the objective lenses.

Eyepiece
Each eyepiece contains lenses that magnify the image. One eyepiece can be adjusted to allow for differences between the eyes.

UP CLOSE
Binoculars are two compact, portable telescopes, side by side. They allow people to see things close up with both eyes.

CLEAR VISION
Glasses are a pair of lenses placed in front of the eyes to correct poor vision.

Double prism
Light rays from the objective lens are reflected by a pair of prisms (glass wedges). The prisms make the binoculars shorter so they are easier to hold steady, and also turn the image the right way up.

Objective lens
This glass lens forms an upside-down image of the object.

HOW LENSES WORK

When light rays travel through a transparent material such as glass, they are slowed down. Light rays usually travel in straight lines, but if they enter the glass at an angle, they change direction. This effect is called refraction. Lenses are shaped to bend light rays in a certain way. There are two types of lenses: concave and convex. Convex lenses bulge in the middle and bend light rays together. The lens in the human eye is a convex lens. Concave lenses are thinnest at their center, and this makes light rays spread out.

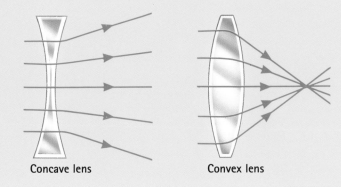

Concave lens   Convex lens

Discover more in Carnival Fun

In Focus

A camera allows us to take photographs of people or scenes. Cameras vary enormously in their complexity but they all operate on the same principle—light enters the camera and falls on the film inside. Light rays enter a camera through a lens, which focuses them to form a sharp image on the film. The camera is aimed by looking through a window called the viewfinder. Many cameras automatically control the amount of light entering them, which makes them simple to use. Other cameras allow you to manually control the amount of light that falls on the film, but this makes them more complicated to use. Some cameras have separate lenses for forming the image on the film and in the viewfinder. One popular type of camera, the single lens reflex (SLR), can have both automatic and manual control. It uses the same lens for both so that the photographer always sees precisely the same scene that will be photographed.

SLR CAMERA
A single lens reflex (SLR) camera can be fitted with a variety of different lenses. A wide-angle lens is used for broad scenes, while a macro lens is added for close-ups. A zoom lens varies the magnifying power.

Winding on
After a photograph is taken, the film winder is turned to move a new piece of film behind the shutter, ready for the next photograph.

Smile!
The shutter release button is pressed to take a photograph.

DID YOU KNOW?
The first permanent photograph was produced in 1827 by Frenchman Joseph-Nicéphore Niépce when he discovered that asphalt was light sensitive. However, posing for his photograph may not have been much fun. He took eight hours to take one photograph!

SINGLE-USE CAMERA
A single-use camera is sold complete with a film loaded inside it. When all the photographs have been taken, the whole camera is sent away for the film to be processed.

Plastic lens
To keep the camera simple to make and use, the plastic lens is set so that it does not have to be adjusted.

Film
A springy plate presses the film into position behind the shutter, and also keeps it flat.

FUN AQUATIC
35 MM CAMERA WITH FILM
Kodak

Viewfinder
The photographer looks through the viewfinder to see the picture the camera will take.

Right way up
The pentaprism is a specially shaped block of glass. It reverses the image formed by the lens so that it appears the correct way through the viewfinder.

MAKING PHOTOGRAPHS

When light falls on photographic film, it causes a chemical reaction in a light-sensitive layer called the emulsion. In the fraction of a second when a camera's shutter is open, the chemical reaction releases a tiny amount of silver from silver crystals in the emulsion. Only a few atoms of silver are released by each crystal, so the image is invisible. When the film is treated with chemicals, millions more silver atoms are released. The emulsion is then washed away in places where light did not fall on it. The picture formed on the film is a negative image—dark where light fell on it. This is turned into a photograph by shining light through the negative onto a sheet of light-sensitive paper and developing the image on the paper. Color film has three layers of light-sensitive chemicals. Each layer is sensitive to a different color. The three colors combine to form a lifelike color photograph.

Hinged mirror
The mirror reflects light entering the camera onto the viewing screen. Once the shutter release is pressed, the mirror flips out of the way to let light fall on the film.

Lens system
The lens in an SLR camera contains several separate lenses that work together to form a clear, sharp image.

HOW A CAMERA SEES
When a photographer presses a camera's shutter release button, the shutter opens and lets light stream in through the lens and fall on the film. The lens focuses the image on the film and a chemical reaction in the film captures the image.

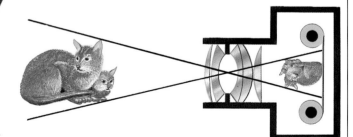

Shutter
The shutter opens to let light fall on the film, then closes again. The time it takes to do this is either set by the photographer or calculated automatically by the camera.

Discover more in Moving Pictures

37

Moving Pictures

Films, like television, rely on "persistence of vision" to trick the viewer into thinking that a series of still pictures is really a single, moving image. A cinema projector flashes 24 frames (pictures) onto a screen every second. They appear to merge together to form a lifelike moving image. If the film was projected by simply running it continuously past a bright light, you would see only a meaningless blur on the screen. The film must be held still while each frame is projected and the light must be cut off while the next frame moves into position. The intense light that shines through the film is cut off by a rotating shutter for a fraction of a second. During this brief moment, a pair of claws seizes the next frame by the holes along its edges and pulls it into position. A lens focuses the image onto the screen.

Exhaust hose
Hot air is blown out of the projector through the exhaust hose.

Lamp
A projector needs a source of intense light to produce a bright image on the screen.

Feed reel
This is a spinning plate that supplies film to the projector.

Fan
An electric fan blows hot air out of the projector to stop it from overheating and damaging the film.

Rotating shutter
This allows light to pass through the film each time a new frame is positioned in front of it.

Take-up reel
After the film passes through the projector, it is wound onto the take-up reel.

Lens
This bends the light rays from the lamp so that they form a sharply focused image on the screen.

Carnival Fun

Feeling funny
When a roller-coaster car dives suddenly, your internal organs take a moment to catch up with the rest of your body. This produces the strange sensation that you are leaving your stomach behind.

Carnival rides are designed to give you surprises, excitement and a sense of danger—even when you know you are safe. The roller coaster is the most thrilling ride of all. A train of cars running on tracks is hauled to the top of the ride and released. Gravity pulls the cars down to the bottom of the track. On the way, the track twists and turns, throwing the cars into violent and unexpected maneuvers—sometimes they even turn upside-down! Computers and modern materials have produced a new generation of higher, faster and more exciting rides. Wooden rides were propped up at the sides with safety supports, which the passengers could see, but modern rides are built on steel frames and do not need side supports. Once you are securely clamped into your seat, you cannot see what is supporting the car, and it seems to fly through the air. Computers constantly monitor the cars and the track to make sure that the ride is safe.

Racing downhill
The slope of the downhill section is carefully calculated to give the cars enough energy to turn, climb, loop the loop and reach the end of the ride without stopping.

Moving Pictures

Films, like television, rely on "persistence of vision" to trick the viewer into thinking that a series of still pictures is really a single, moving image. A cinema projector flashes 24 frames (pictures) onto a screen every second. They appear to merge together to form a lifelike moving image. If the film was projected by simply running it continuously past a bright light, you would see only a meaningless blur on the screen. The film must be held still while each frame is projected and the light must be cut off while the next frame moves into position. The intense light that shines through the film is cut off by a rotating shutter for a fraction of a second. During this brief moment, a pair of claws seizes the next frame by the holes along its edges and pulls it into position. A lens focuses the image onto the screen.

Exhaust hose
Hot air is blown out of the projector through the exhaust hose.

Lamp
A projector needs a source of intense light to produce a bright image on the screen.

Feed reel
This is a spinning plate that supplies film to the projector.

Fan
An electric fan blows hot air out of the projector to stop it from overheating and damaging the film.

Rotating shutter
This allows light to pass through the film each time a new frame is positioned in front of it.

Take-up reel
After the film passes through the projector, it is wound onto the take-up reel.

Lens
This bends the light rays from the lamp so that they form a sharply focused image on the screen.

38

Viewfinder
The photographer looks through the viewfinder to see the picture the camera will take.

Right way up
The pentaprism is a specially shaped block of glass. It reverses the image formed by the lens so that it appears the correct way through the viewfinder.

MAKING PHOTOGRAPHS

When light falls on photographic film, it causes a chemical reaction in a light-sensitive layer called the emulsion. In the fraction of a second when a camera's shutter is open, the chemical reaction releases a tiny amount of silver from silver crystals in the emulsion. Only a few atoms of silver are released by each crystal, so the image is invisible. When the film is treated with chemicals, millions more silver atoms are released. The emulsion is then washed away in places where light did not fall on it. The picture formed on the film is a negative image—dark where light fell on it. This is turned into a photograph by shining light through the negative onto a sheet of light-sensitive paper and developing the image on the paper. Color film has three layers of light-sensitive chemicals. Each layer is sensitive to a different color. The three colors combine to form a lifelike color photograph.

Hinged mirror
The mirror reflects light entering the camera onto the viewing screen. Once the shutter release is pressed, the mirror flips out of the way to let light fall on the film.

Lens system
The lens in an SLR camera contains several separate lenses that work together to form a clear, sharp image.

HOW A CAMERA SEES

When a photographer presses a camera's shutter release button, the shutter opens and lets light stream in through the lens and fall on the film. The lens focuses the image on the film and a chemical reaction in the film captures the image.

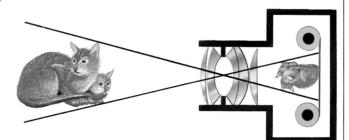

Shutter
The shutter opens to let light fall on the film, then closes again. The time it takes to do this is either set by the photographer or calculated automatically by the camera.

Discover more in Moving Pictures

37

LOOPING THE LOOP

Roller coasters hurl you up, down and around. If the cars are traveling upside-down, the sheer force of their speed carries them forward, but at the same time the curve of the track also pulls them inward. The cars push back against the rails and stay firmly on the track and the passengers are pushed into their seats instead of falling out.

Wheels
The cars are clamped to the track so they cannot fly off.

DID YOU KNOW?

The roller-coaster ride can be traced back to ice slides in Russia in the seventeenth century. The popularity of downhill rides spread from Russia to France, where people put wheels on the sleds so that they could enjoy rides in places where there was no ice. The modern roller-coaster ride with cars on twisting, turning tracks began in the United States at the end of the nineteenth century.

SOUND SYSTEM

The soundtrack is printed on the edge of the film. A light shines through the film's edge and the varying brightness of the light passing through the soundtrack is detected by a photoelectric cell on the other side. This produces an electric current, which is amplified and sent to speakers all around the theater.

ANIMATION AT WORK

Animated films are made frame by frame, and each frame is slightly different from the one before it. When the frames are projected at a rate of 24 per second, they blend to form a single, moving picture. An animated cartoon consists of thousands of separate pictures. Each one is drawn and painted on clear plastic film and photographed separately. Animated puppet films are made by photographing the puppets, then moving them slightly for the next photograph, and so on. Computers can now produce images of very high quality, and these are sometimes included in animated films, or even used for entire films.

Recording Sound

Recorded sound enables us to listen to music wherever and whenever we like. Recordings can be broadcast to millions of people by radio. Small, lightweight personal stereos and compact disk players allow us to enjoy music in private, even while we are on the move. Most recorded sound depends on either magnetism or light. Personal stereos and tape recorders use magnetism. Before sound can be recorded magnetically, it must first be changed into an electrical signal by a microphone. The electrical signal is then changed into a varying magnetic force that magnetizes the recording tape. Compact disk players use light. Sound is stored on the silver-colored disk as a pattern of tiny pits (holes). When light bounces off the spinning disk, the pits make the reflections vary. The varying intensity of the reflections is changed into electricity, and a speaker then converts this into sound.

PORTABLE PERSONAL STEREO
A personal stereo is a miniature tape recorder. The pattern of magnetism on the tape creates a varying current in the playback head next to the tape. The current is amplified (made larger) and then changed into sound by the earphones.

Spindles
The portable stereo contains two spindles. They wind the tape from one spool to the other, past the tape heads.

Playback head
This detects the magnetic pattern on the tape and changes it into an electric current.

HOW MAGNETIC TAPE WORKS

The record head and playback head of a tape recorder are electromagnets. The strength of the magnetic field set up by the record head varies as the current through it varies. As the tape moves past the head when recording, parts of the tape are magnetized to varying degrees. When the magnetized tape is run past the playback head, the fluctuating magnetism from the tape sets up tiny currents in a coil of wire. These are then amplified and fed to the headphones or to the speaker.

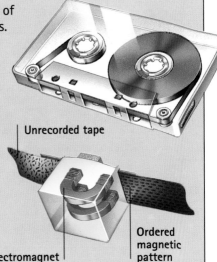

Unrecorded tape

Electromagnet

Ordered magnetic pattern

Rails
Sensors positioned at regular intervals along the steel rails signal computers to close down the ride if they detect any problems.

DODGEM CARS

Dodgems are electric bumper cars. Electric current flows from an overhead mesh and down the pole at the back of each car to the motor that drives the wheels. Rubber bumpers protect the cars from damage when they collide.

Safety equipment
The passengers are held safely in their seats by steel bars covered with soft, spongy material.

Station
Rides begin and end at a station on a straight, level section of track.

Recording Sound

Recorded sound enables us to listen to music wherever and whenever we like. Recordings can be broadcast to millions of people by radio. Small, lightweight personal stereos and compact disk players allow us to enjoy music in private, even while we are on the move. Most recorded sound depends on either magnetism or light. Personal stereos and tape recorders use magnetism. Before sound can be recorded magnetically, it must first be changed into an electrical signal by a microphone. The electrical signal is then changed into a varying magnetic force that magnetizes the recording tape. Compact disk players use light. Sound is stored on the silver-colored disk as a pattern of tiny pits (holes). When light bounces off the spinning disk, the pits make the reflections vary. The varying intensity of the reflections is changed into electricity, and a speaker then converts this into sound.

COMPACT DISK PLAYER
A compact disk player is a machine that uses light, produced by a laser, to react to a spiral pattern of tiny holes in a spinning plastic disk.

PORTABLE PERSONAL STEREO
A personal stereo is a miniature tape recorder. The pattern of magnetism on the tape creates a varying current in the playback head next to the tape. The current is amplified (made larger) and then changed into sound by the earphones.

Spindles
The portable stereo contains two spindles. They wind the tape from one spool to the other, past the tape heads.

Playback head
This detects the magnetic pattern on the tape and changes it into an electric current.

How Magnetic Tape Works

The record head and playback head of a tape recorder are electromagnets. The strength of the magnetic field set up by the record head varies as the current through it varies. As the tape moves past the head when recording, parts of the tape are magnetized to varying degrees. When the magnetized tape is run past the playback head, the fluctuating magnetism from the tape sets up tiny currents in a coil of wire. These are then amplified and fed to the headphones or to the speaker.

Unrecorded tape

Electromagnet

Ordered magnetic pattern

44

SOUND SYSTEM

The soundtrack is printed on the edge of the film. A light shines through the film's edge and the varying brightness of the light passing through the soundtrack is detected by a photoelectric cell on the other side. This produces an electric current, which is amplified and sent to speakers all around the theater.

STRANGE BUT TRUE

The first motion pictures were made by Louis Aimé Augustin Le Prince in 1888. In 1890, Le Prince set off from Dijon in France to demonstrate his invention in New York. But he never arrived, and no trace of him was ever found.

ANIMATION AT WORK

Animated films are made frame by frame, and each frame is slightly different from the one before it. When the frames are projected at a rate of 24 per second, they blend to form a single, moving picture. An animated cartoon consists of thousands of separate pictures. Each one is drawn and painted on clear plastic film and photographed separately. Animated puppet films are made by photographing the puppets, then moving them slightly for the next photograph, and so on. Computers can now produce images of very high quality, and these are sometimes included in animated films, or even used for entire films.

MIRROR, MIRROR

Some mirrors curve inward and outward. They distort reflections and make people look shorter and fatter, or taller and thinner, than they really are.

Concave mirror
This curves inward and makes you look taller and thinner.

Convex mirror
This curves outward and makes you look shorter and fatter.

WALL OF DEATH

The wall of death allows people to hang in midair as if by magic. They stand around the inside of a wall and a motor spins the room around. The spinning motion pushes them against the wall so that when the floor is lowered they do not fall.

Room starts to spin

Room spinning and floor lowered

IN A SPIN

Roller coasters can turn upside-down without tipping the passengers out. The curve of the track is carefully designed so that the passengers are pushed into their seats when the cars turn upside-down. When a vehicle follows a curved path, the people inside it feel themselves being pushed toward the outside of the curve. To see this effect, take a bucket outside and put a small amount of water in the bottom (Step 1). When you whirl the bucket around like a roller coaster looping the loop (Step 2), the water tries to fly away from you, but pulling the bucket around in a circle presses the water against the base of the bucket.

Step 1

Step 2

DID YOU KNOW?

The first sound recording was made by shouting at a diaphragm—a disk that vibrates in response to the sound waves of a voice. As the disk vibrated, it activated a needle attached to it. This scored a groove in a spinning cylinder covered with tinfoil. When the recording was played back, the groove made the needle and disk vibrate and recreate the voice.

MICROPHONE
Performers often wear radio microphones. The microphone changes the performer's voice into an electrical signal. Then a battery-powered radio transmitter, sometimes worn on a belt, sends it to a radio receiver, which relays it to the audience via the sound system.

Making music
On a circuit board beneath this casing, the Digital to Analog Converter (DAC) changes pulses of electricity from the photodiode (a light-sensitive conductor) into an analog (smoothly varying) electrical signal. When this is amplified, a speaker changes it into a copy of the sound recorded on the compact disk.

Laser
The laser produces an intense beam of light. A lens focuses this beam onto a spot on the disk that is one millionth of a yard across.

Photodiode
This converts reflections from the disk into an electrical signal.

THE PITS
A standard compact disk, 5 in (12 cm) across and just over $1/25$ in (1 mm) thick, can hold an hour of music. It is covered with a spiral pattern of microscopic pits. Each pit is invisible to the naked eye.

Discover more in Music to Our Ears

45

Music to Our Ears

A symphony orchestra fills a concert hall with music. From the piccolo to the double bass, all musical instruments produce sound in the same way—they make the air vibrate. Some wind instruments have woody reeds or rely on the players' lips to make the air vibrate; in others, such as the flute, the vibration comes from the players' breath passing over the sharp edge of a hole in the instrument. Stringed instruments use vibrating strings, while percussion instruments vibrate when they are struck. The first vibration from a reed or a string is usually very weak, so most instruments have a way to make more air vibrate, which in turn makes the sound louder. Stringed instruments, for example, have a sounding board that vibrates with the strings and amplifies the sound. Some percussion instruments, such as the xylophone, have hollow tubes or blocks of wood to increase the sound they make. Although musical instruments produce sound in the same way, they do not produce the same sounds. Instruments are all shapes and sizes and are made from a variety of materials. The music they make is just as varied.

PLAYING THE PIANO

A piano has wire strings that are stretched tightly in pairs or groups over an iron frame. Each set of strings has a hammer. When the player strikes the keys, strongly or gently, the hammer strikes the strings with the same force and makes them vibrate. The long strings make low notes and the short strings make high notes. When the air around the strings vibrates, a sounding board behind them amplifies the sound. The angled lid of a grand piano deflects the sound toward the audience.

PAN PIPES
When you blow across the top of a pipe, the air inside vibrates and produces a musical note. A long pipe holds more air and makes a lower note than a short pipe.

Black and white
The keyboard of a piano has 52 white keys and 36 black keys.

BOTTLED MUSIC

Tap a bottle and listen to the sound it makes. If you pour some water into the bottle, the amount of air inside is reduced and the pitch of the sound is raised. You can make your own version of a xylophone by setting out a line of bottles and filling them with different amounts of water. Tap the bottles gently with a pencil and notice the different sound each bottle makes. You can tune your xylophone by adding or pouring out water in each bottle.

Pedals
Foot pedals change the length and loudness of a note. The pedal on the right lifts all the dampers so the sound continues after the key has been released. The pedal on the left moves the hammers sideways, to make the sound softer. Some pianos have a third (middle) pedal. This sustains notes that are already sounding when the pedal is pressed.

INTO THE BEAT

A drum has a skin stretched across the top, which vibrates when hit. A tight skin vibrates faster and makes a higher note than a loose skin.

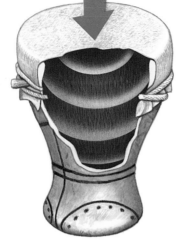

Frame

The strings are stretched over an iron frame. If this frame were to bend, the notes produced by the strings would change and the piano would be out of tune.

In tune

The piano is tuned by adjusting special tuning pins. These can change the pitch of the note.

Strings

The strings are made of steel wire. The higher notes are made by groups of two or three short, thin strings. The lower notes are made by a long, thick string.

String

The string is held down by the damper until the hammer rises.

Damper

The felt-covered damper stops the string from vibrating.

Hammer

A felt-covered hammer is raised to strike the string.

Key

The key is a lever. The player presses one end and this raises the other end to make the hammer move.

PRESSING THE KEYS

When a piano player presses the keys, a complicated set of levers and catches is set in motion, as shown here.

Discover more in Recording Sound

47

The World in View

Television programs are usually transmitted to your home by radio waves, but they can also travel via underground cables. Your rooftop antenna detects the radio waves and converts them into an electrical signal. The television converts this signal into pictures and sound. A television picture seems to be moving, but it is really a technological trick that fools your eyes and brain. The picture on the screen is made by a glowing spot that moves from side to side and up and down so quickly that the whole screen seems to glow at the same time. Television pictures appear on the screen one after another so rapidly that they look like a single moving picture. It works because of an effect called "persistence of vision." When light forms an image (picture) on the retina (the light-sensitive layer at the back of your eye), the image stays on the retina for a fraction of a second after the light that formed it has gone. This means that when images reach your eyes very quickly, one after the other, they merge together.

Video drum
The video drum spins at an angle to the tape. Tape heads (small electromagnets) on the surface of the video drum transfer the electrical signals into a magnetic pattern on the video tape.

Video cassette
When a standard video cassette is put into the recorder, the machine automatically opens a flap on the front edge, pulls out a loop of tape, and wraps this around the video drum.

TELEVISION
A television converts electrical signals from a rooftop antenna or an underground cable into pictures and sound. This is a widescreen television. Its screen is one-third wider than a normal television.

Screen
The television screen, on which pictures are formed, is the flattened end of a large glass tube.

Phosphors
The back of the screen is coated with chemicals called "phosphors." They glow in one of three colors—red, green or blue—when electrons strike them.

Shadow mask
The shadow mask is a metal sheet with slots in it, and three electron beams pass through it on their way to the screen. The mask ensures that each electron beam strikes and lights up only one phosphor: red, green or blue.

VIDEO CASSETTE RECORDER
A video cassette recorder can record television programs by storing the electrical signals from the television antenna magnetically on video tape.

48

DID YOU KNOW?

When televisions first went on sale they were sold as kits. The buyer had to put the television together. The screen was often only 4 in (10 cm) high and 2 in (5 cm) wide.

Electron beams
Three beams of electrons fly from the back of the tube to the screen. Electric fields focus them onto the screen.

Deflection coils
Electromagnets around the neck of the tube deflect (bend) the beams from side to side as well as up and down to trace out the pattern of horizontal lines that form the picture.

REMOTE CONTROL

When buttons on the remote control handset are pressed, an invisible infrared beam sends instructions to the television. The beam is a stream of coded pulses. This tells the television which buttons were pressed and what to do next.

IN COLOR

A television can produce a picture that contains all the colors in the rainbow. The phosphors on the back of the screen that produce the picture, however, glow in only three colors—red, green and blue. Every color can be made by mixing different amounts of red, green and blue light. For this reason, they are called primary colors. Mixing these primary colors together in precisely the correct proportions produces white light. The glowing colored spots on a television screen are so small and so close together that, from a distance, they appear to merge together to form different colors.

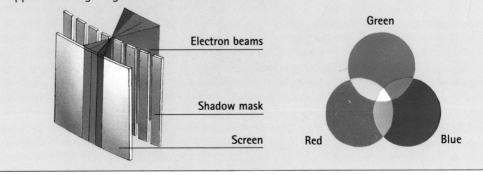

Electron beams

Shadow mask

Screen

Green

Red

Blue

Discover more in Keeping in Touch

49

On the Road Again

When Carl Benz visualized the "horseless carriage" last century he could not have imagined how complex cars would become. Modern cars consist of several different mechanical and electrical systems all working together. The fuel system supplies fuel to the engine, and the ignition system provides electrical sparks at just the right moment to ignite the fuel. The transmission system transmits the power generated by the engine to the car's wheels. The lubrication system keeps all the moving parts in the engine covered with a film of oil so that they can slip over each other without sticking. The cooling system stops the engine from overheating and the braking system stops the car safely. The suspension system allows the wheels to follow bumps and dips in the road while the rest of the car glides along smoothly. Today there are more than 400 million passenger cars on roads around the world.

Suspension
A system of springs and oil-filled telescopic tubes called dampers absorbs bumps in the road and gives a smoother ride.

Brake cables
Brake cables are connected to levers on the handlebars. When the levers are squeezed, the cables compress the brake pads on the wheels and slow the bicycle down.

Fuel tank
The fuel that is burned in the engine is pumped from a tank at the rear of the car.

Tires
Pneumatic (air-filled) tires give a smoother ride over small bumps in the ground.

STRANGE BUT TRUE

In 1865, a law was passed in England to limit the speed of steam cars. They were not allowed to go faster than 2 miles (3 km) per hour in cities and they also had to travel behind a man waving a red flag!

Chain
The chain passes around the gears and turns the rear wheel.

Gears
Gears make a bicycle easier to pedal. Low gears turn the wheel only a small amount and help the rider to pedal uphill.

Spokes
Thin wire spokes hold the wheels in place and let the wind blow through them instead of against the bicycle.

Gear shift
In a manual vehicle, the driver changes gear by moving the gear shift.

Air filter
Dust and dirt in the air are trapped in this filter to prevent them from being sucked into the engine.

Engine
Fuel is pumped from the tank to the carburetor or a fuel injection system, which vaporizes the fuel. An explosive mixture of air and vapor is sucked into the cylinders and burned to move pistons. The pistons turn the wheels.

CONTROLLING TRAFFIC

Traffic lights control vehicles at major road junctions. The same code of lights, though not the same signals, is used all over the world. A red light means stop, and a green light means that it is safe to go. A yellow light warns drivers that the lights are about to change color. Some traffic lights automatically change color after a certain interval. Computerized lights can tell how many vehicles have passed by and they change according to the volume of traffic. A loop of wire buried in the road carries an electric current that creates a magnetic field. When a vehicle passes over the loop, it distorts the magnetic field. This is sensed by a roadside computer, which is programmed to change the traffic lights.

Alternator
The alternator generates nearly all the electricity the car's systems need and keeps the battery fully charged.

Battery
The battery starts the engine and supplies electricity for the engine's electrical system.

Distributor
The distributor sends a charge of electricity to a spark plug in each cylinder, and this ignites the fuel inside.

Radiator
Water for cooling the engine is pumped through the radiator to cool it down before it returns to the engine.

Fan
The fan, driven by the engine or by a separate electric motor, sucks air through the radiator to cool down the water as it flows through.

Disk brakes
When the driver presses the brake pedal, tough pads grip the disk that turns with the wheel and slows it down.

Discover more in Riding on Air

51

RAILWAY SIGNALS

Colored light signals by the side of the track tell train drivers whether or not it is safe for a train to proceed.

A green signal indicates that two or more sections of track ahead of a train are clear and it is safe to proceed.

A yellow signal indicates that only one clear section of track separates two trains. As a train passes each signal, it changes to red.

A red signal shows that the track ahead is not clear and an alarm sounds in the driver's cab.

When the train has stopped, the alarm continues to sound a warning that it is not safe to proceed.

Staying on Track

If you travel anywhere by train, your carriage will be pulled along by one of four types of locomotive. In a few places, steam locomotives are still used. Coal is burned to heat water and make steam, which pushes pistons inside cylinders to turn the wheels. Diesel or diesel-electric locomotives are now more common than steam engines. Diesel locomotives burn oil in a piston engine, which is like a giant car engine, to turn the wheels. Diesel-electric locomotives use a diesel engine to drive an electric generator. The generator powers the electric motors that turn the wheels. The world's fastest railway trains are pulled by electric locomotives that convert electrical energy directly into movement. The electricity for the motors is supplied by cables suspended over the track. The German InterCity Express (ICE) train is one of the world's fastest trains: its top speed is more than 248 miles (400 km) per hour, but it usually transports passengers at 155 miles (250 km) per hour.

ICE TRAIN
The German ICE (InterCity Express) is an example of a modern, high-speed electric train.

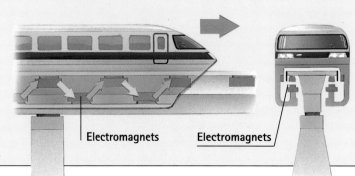

FLYING ON MAGNETISM

The maglev (magnetic levitation train) is held above its track, or guideway, by powerful forces between electromagnets (electrically powered magnets) in the track and in the train. Magnets in the sides of the train hold it steady in the guideway. Magnetic fields are also used to make the train move. Magnets ahead of the train attract it, pulling it forward, and magnets behind repel it, pushing it forward. The magnetic field ripples along the guideway, pulling the train with it. There is no contact between the train and the track and passengers have a very smooth and quiet ride.

British maglev train

Close behind
These carriages are divided into sections with seats in rows or facing each other.

Riding up front
The carriages at the front have fewer seats and more room than those behind.

Electromagnets　　**Electromagnets**

Catenary wire
This holds up the power supply line.

Power supply line
This is suspended from the catenary wire so that it is level and does not sag.

Driver controls
Information collected from the motors and carriages is sent to the cockpit instruments by optical fibers. This information helps the driver control the train.

Streamlined body
The smooth lines of the train's body enable it to slip through the air as easily as possible.

Pantograph
This is a frame that extends from the top of the locomotive and touches the power line above the track. Electric current flows from the power line through conductors in the pantograph to the locomotive's electric motors.

DID YOU KNOW?
The width of modern railway tracks is based on the distance between the wheels of horse-drawn carts that were used nearly 200 years ago. The distance between a pair of rails is called the gauge of the track. A locomotive made for one gauge cannot travel on the track of a different gauge.

Traction motor
This is an electric motor that drives the locomotive's wheels.

• TRANSPORTATION •

Roaming the Oceans

When anything tries to move through water, the water resists its movement. Boat designers try to minimize water resistance, called "drag," by making boat hulls as smooth and streamlined as possible. Water underneath a boat pushes up against its hull with a force called "upthrust." If the force of the boat's weight is equal to the upthrust of the water, the boat floats. If the boat weighs more than the upthrust of the water, it sinks. A submarine, or a smaller underwater craft called a submersible, sinks under the waves by letting water into its ballast tanks to make it heavier. It rises to the surface again by forcing the water out of the tanks with compressed air, or by dropping heavy weights to make the craft lighter. Most working boats, submarines and submersibles are powered by propellers with angled blades that push against the water as they turn.

Manipulator arm
A robot arm with a mechanical claw at the end of it picks up objects from the sea bed.

SETTING SAIL
A sail is set at an angle so that wind blowing around the sail from the side reduces the air pressure in front of it, sucking the sail and the boat forward. This means that a sail can use a wind blowing in one direction to propel a yacht in a completely different direction. But a yacht can never sail directly into the wind.

BELOW THE SURFACE
Submersibles allow scientists to explore the sea bed, study living organisms in their natural surroundings and investigate shipwrecks.

Thruster
A thruster is a propeller inside a tube driven by an electric motor. Submersibles are propelled and steered by thrusters.

Ballast tanks
The submersible sinks by letting water into its ballast tanks.

Batteries
Electric power for the thrusters, lights, cameras and other instruments is supplied by a set of batteries.

Iron ballast
Iron bars provide some of the weight that is required to sink the submersible.

GLOBAL POSITIONING SYSTEM

Navigators used to figure out the position of a ship at sea by studying the position of the sun or the stars. Now they use a system called "Global Positioning System" (GPS). Satellites orbiting the Earth send out radio signals that are picked up by a receiver in the ship. The signals tell the receiver where each satellite is, how fast it is flying, in which direction and what the time is. By using signals from at least three satellites, the receiver can calculate the position of the ship.

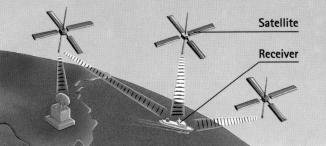

Satellite

Receiver

GPS display unit

Crew sphere
The crew members sit inside a metal sphere because a sphere is the best shape to resist the crushing pressure of water. Air for the crew to breathe is also stored in spherical tanks.

Discover more in Riding on Air

55

LIFT
The wings are pulled upward by the difference in pressure above and below them.

THRUST
This is the force that the engines produce to drive the plane forward.

AIRBUS A340
This airplane is specifically designed for long-range flights. It has four engines and can carry large amounts of fuel.

• TRANSPORTATION •

Riding on Air

The Airbus A340 weighs up to 553,000 lb (251,000 kg). It looks as if it could not possibly fly, yet when it reaches a speed of up to 183 miles (295 km) per hour, its nose tips up and it soars skyward. Airplanes are able to fly because of the shape of their wings. Air is forced to travel over the curved top of the wings farther and faster than it can move past the flat underside. This has the effect of lowering the air pressure above the wings. The difference in pressure above and below the wings sucks the wings upward. When this force, called "lift," is greater than the weight of the airplane, the plane takes off. The airplane has moving panels in the wings (ailerons) and in the tail (the elevators or rudder). When these "control surfaces" are moved, the air pushing against them makes the plane turn or climb or dive.

WEIGHT
The weight of the plane is the effect of gravity pulling it down to Earth.

Parachute vent
To make the balloon descend, a cord is pulled to open a vent at the top of the balloon. The hot air that escapes through it is replaced by cool air, which makes the balloon heavier.

Envelope
The envelope is usually made from plastic-coated nylon, which cannot tear.

HOT-AIR BALLOON
A hot-air balloon rises because the hot air inside it is lighter than the cooler air outside the balloon.

Gas burner
The air in the balloon is heated by a gas flame from a propane gas burner.

56

Slats
Slats are strips that extend from the front of the wings to generate more lift and adapt the plane for flying at lower speeds.

On the inside
Spars (metal beams) running the length of the wings are linked by ribs running from front to back, forming a very strong structure.

Flaps
Flaps are panels that extend from the rear of the wings and function in the same way as slats.

Engine
This works when air is sucked into the engine through a large spinning fan. Fuel is mixed with air and burned in the combustion chamber. Hot gases then rush out of the engine through the exhaust nozzle, creating the force to drive the plane forward.

Rudder
Turning the rudder pushes the plane's tail out to the left or right.

Combustion chamber

Exhaust nozzle

Fan

Wheels
When the plane is airborne, the wheels fold up into the body.

Cabin
The passenger cabin is pressurized by air pumps to provide enough oxygen for the passengers to breathe.

DRAG
This force is caused by air resistance that tries to slow the plane down.

HOW RADAR WORKS

Pulses of radio waves are sent out from a radar transmitter. Large metal objects in the path of the waves, such as an airplane, reflect the waves. Some of the waves travel back to the dish where a receiver detects them. The time they take to be reflected from an airplane can be measured very accurately. As radio waves are known to travel at the speed of light, the distance to the airplane can be calculated. The plane's position is shown as a glowing spot on a radar screen.

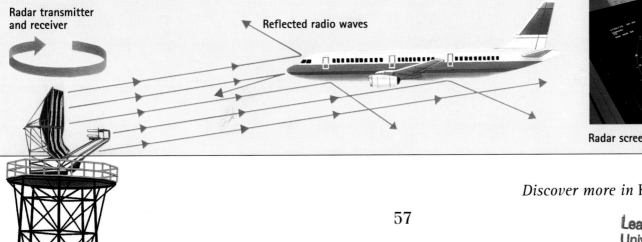

Radar transmitter and receiver

Reflected radio waves

Radar screen

Discover more in Reaching into Space

Reaching into Space

Technology has made it possible for us to reach into space. Special engines, for example, have been designed to power spacecraft in this airless environment. Fuel needs oxygen to burn, but because there is no oxygen in space, the rockets that propel spacecraft carry their own supply of oxygen, or a substance containing oxygen, which is mixed with the fuel before it is burned. When rocket fuel is burned, the hot gases produced expand rapidly and rush out through a nozzle. The force propels the spacecraft in the opposite direction. When the nozzle is turned, the jet of gases changes direction and this steers the rocket. In the early days of space travel, rockets and spacecraft could be used once only. In 1981, however, America launched a reusable space shuttle. It consists of an orbiter space-plane, two booster rockets and an external fuel tank. The orbiter takes off like a rocket, glides back from space, and lands on a runway, like an aircraft.

Flight deck
The orbiter is controlled by its commander and pilot from the flight deck.

Thermal tiles
Tiles cover the orbiter to protect it from the intense heat it encounters when it re-enters the atmosphere.

FLIGHT OF THE SPACE SHUTTLE
Unlike early spacecraft, the space shuttle can be reused. After each flight, it is checked and prepared for another launch.

The orbiter's engines propel it into orbit.

A satellite is launched from the payload bay.

The empty external fuel tank is dropped.

The orbiter's engines fire to begin its descent.

The rocket boosters fall away.

The orbiter glows red hot as it plunges through the atmosphere.

Take off

The orbiter glides down toward the runway.

The space shuttle is prepared for take off.

Touchdown

SPACE SHUTTLE

Two astronauts check a satellite before it is launched from the space shuttle orbiter's payload bay. They are linked to the orbiter by safety lines so they cannot float away into space. Small satellites are released into space by springs. Larger satellites are lifted out of the payload bay by the orbiter's robot arm. At a safe distance from the orbiter, the satellite's rocket thrusters fire to boost it into the correct orbit.

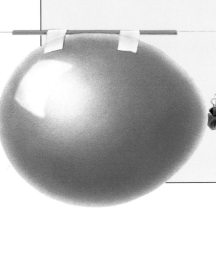

TAKE OFF!

You can make your own rocket with a balloon. Blow up a balloon and clip it closed. Attach a drinking straw to the balloon with tape. Pass a length of thread through the straw and tie it tightly to two chairs placed 7 ft (2 m) apart from each other. Launch your rocket by taking the clip off the balloon. Air rushes out of the balloon and pushes it in the opposite direction.

Orbital maneuvering engines
Two engines in the orbiter's tail move it to a higher or lower orbit and begin its descent at the end of the mission.

Robot arm
The orbiter is equipped with a robot arm for moving satellites and experiments into and out of the payload bay.

Thrusters
Changes to the orbiter's position are made by firing rocket thrusters contained in its nose and tail.

Payload bay
Satellites and even fully equipped scientific laboratories can be carried in the payload bay, which is 59 ft (18 m) long and 16 ft (5 m) across.

Main engines
The three main engines, supplied with fuel from an external tank, are fired for the first 8½ minutes of each flight.

The Principles of Things

All machines, instruments and electronic devices, from a humble office stapler or a magnifying glass to a computer or the space shuttle, make use of scientific principles. Understanding a few basic scientific principles can make it easier to see why machines are built the way they are, why some machines have a certain shape and how they work.

Equal air pressure

Lower air pressure in straw

Adequate oxygen supply

Reduced oxygen supply

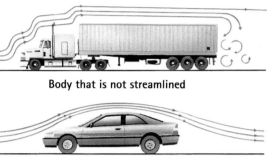

Body that is not streamlined

Streamlined body

Aerodynamics

This is the study of how air flows around objects. An object's shape affects the way that air flows around it. Air does not flow easily around a broad, angular shape, such as a truck, but it does flow easily around a slim, smoothly curved shape, such as a car. Such an object is said to be streamlined. Streamlining is particularly important for racing cars, jet airliners, rockets or anything else designed to travel at high speed.

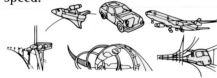

Air pressure

Air pressure describes the way that air pushes back when it is squeezed. Air pressure is greatest near the Earth's surface because of the air above pressing down. High above the Earth, the air pressure is low. When you use a drinking straw you use air pressure. Sucking air out of the straw lowers the air pressure inside. The higher air pressure outside forces the drink up the straw to fill the lower pressure area.

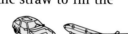

Combustion

Combustion is another word for burning. It is a chemical reaction that gives out heat and light in the form of a flame. It occurs when a substance reacts quickly with oxygen, a gas in the air around us. A burning candle underneath an upturned glass soon uses up the oxygen in the air trapped under the glass. Its flame shrinks and goes out, while a candle outside the glass would continue to burn.

Electromagnetic radiation

Light, radio and X-rays are all examples of electromagnetic radiation. They consist of waves of electric and magnetic energy vibrating through space. The only difference between them is the length of the waves. Light is the only part of the electromagnetic spectrum that our eyes can detect. The whole spectrum is shown below, with wavelengths given in meters. Each wavelength is ten times the one before it; 10^3 meters is the same as 10 x 10 x 10, or 1,000 meters.

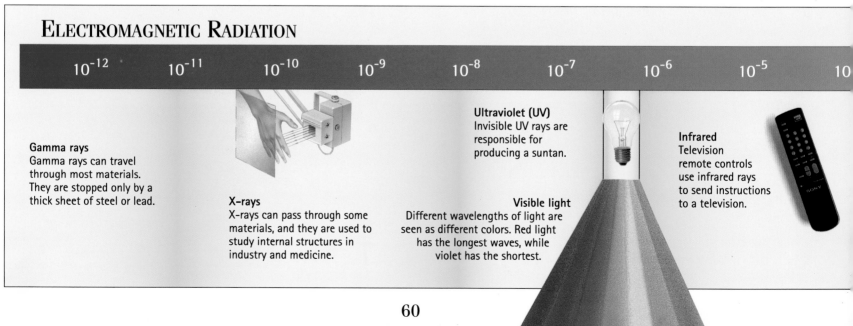

ELECTROMAGNETIC RADIATION

10^{-12} 10^{-11} 10^{-10} 10^{-9} 10^{-8} 10^{-7} 10^{-6} 10^{-5} 10

Gamma rays
Gamma rays can travel through most materials. They are stopped only by a thick sheet of steel or lead.

X-rays
X-rays can pass through some materials, and they are used to study internal structures in industry and medicine.

Ultraviolet (UV)
Invisible UV rays are responsible for producing a suntan.

Visible light
Different wavelengths of light are seen as different colors. Red light has the longest waves, while violet has the shortest.

Infrared
Television remote controls use infrared rays to send instructions to a television.

Gravity

Gravity is the force that pulls everything toward the ground, such as an apple falling from a tree. Gravity also makes the moon circle the Earth and the Earth circle the sun. The strength of an object's gravity depends on the amount of matter it is made from. Stars have a stronger gravitational pull than planets, because stars are bigger than planets.

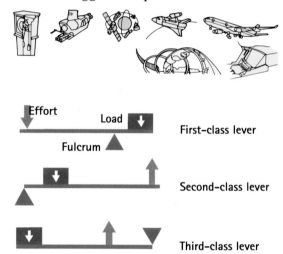

Levers

A lever is a device that transfers a force from one place to somewhere else. Every lever has a load, an effort and a fulcrum. The effort makes the lever pivot at the fulcrum, moving the load. There are three different ways of arranging the effort, load and fulcrum, called three classes of lever. A first-class lever is like a see-saw, a second-class lever is like a wheelbarrow and a third-class lever is like your own forearm.

Magnetism

Magnetism is a force produced by magnets, which can attract materials such as iron, steel, cobalt and nickel. A bar magnet has a north pole and a south pole. If a north pole is brought close to the south pole of another magnet, they attract each other. If two north poles or two south poles are brought together, they push each other away. Magnetism is also produced when electricity flows. An electric current flowing along a wire creates a magnetic field around the wire.

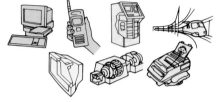

Reflection

When a wave strikes a surface it bounces back, like a ball bouncing off a wall. This rebounding effect is called reflection. We can see ourselves in a mirror because light waves are reflected by the mirror.

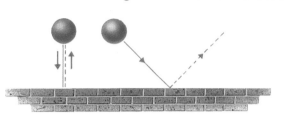

Refraction

When light travels from one substance into another, such as from air to water, it changes speed and direction. This is called refraction. A wedge of glass called a prism separates light into all the colors it contains by refraction. The different colors present in sunlight are bent by different amounts, so the colors separate and form a rainbow.

Light

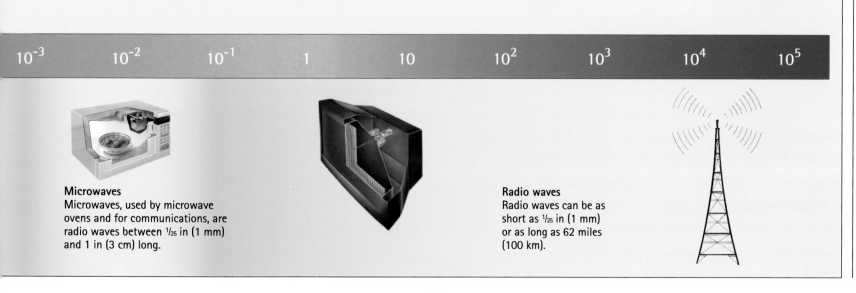

10^{-3} 10^{-2} 10^{-1} 1 10 10^2 10^3 10^4 10^5

Microwaves
Microwaves, used by microwave ovens and for communications, are radio waves between 1/25 in (1 mm) and 1 in (3 cm) long.

Radio waves
Radio waves can be as short as 1/25 in (1 mm) or as long as 62 miles (100 km).

Glossary

Barcode scanner

Binoculars

Pan flute

Viking space probe

Vacuum cleaner

amplitude The size of a wave. A sound wave with a large amplitude is louder than a sound wave with a small amplitude.

antenna A device that receives or transmits radio waves. An antenna connected to a radio receiver changes radio waves into electrical signals. An antenna connected to a radio transmitter changes electrical signals into radio waves.

Archimedes' screw A device used to raise liquids. It consists of a screw inside a pipe. As the screw is turned, the water rises up inside the pipe.

atom A particle of matter. It is the smallest existing part of an element.

ballast A weight used to stabilize a ship, submersible or submarine.

barcode A pattern of lines containing information about a product. The information is read by pointing a laser at the barcode to detect the varying reflections.

block and tackle Several pulleys linked together to make it easier to lift a heavy weight. The top set of pulleys is the block and the lower set is the tackle.

carrier wave A radio wave used to carry information, such as a radio program.

CD-ROM Compact disk read-only memory. A compact disk designed to store computer data.

compact disk (CD) A disk on which music or other sounds are recorded as a pattern of microscopic pits. The disk is played by bouncing a laser beam off it and turning the pattern of pits into sound.

concave lens A lens that is thinner in the middle than at the edges.

convex lens A lens that is thicker in the middle than at the edges.

data Information. Computer data may include numbers, text, sound or pictures.

disk drive The part of a computer that is used to read or write data.

drag A force that tries to slow down anything moving through air or water.

electromagnetic wave A wave of energy made of vibrating electric and magnetic fields. Light, radio and X-rays are examples of electromagnetic waves.

electron A particle of matter with a negative electric charge found in an atom. Electrons moving in the same direction form an electric current.

emulsion The light-sensitive coating on photographic film.

escapement The part of a clock or watch that regulates its speed.

eyepiece The lens or group of lenses nearest the eye in a microscope, telescope or pair of binoculars.

fax machine A facsimile machine. A machine used to send and receive documents by telephone.

fiber-optic cable A cable made from hair-thin strands of pure glass.

filament A thin wire inside a bulb. The filament glows when an electric current flows through it.

floppy disk A magnetic disk used for recording computer data.

fluorescent tube A tube that glows when an electric current passes through the gas inside.

focus The point where light rays bent by a lens come together.

frequency The rate of vibration of any wavelike motion including light, radio or water waves.

gravity The force that pulls us down to the ground and also keeps the Earth and the other planets circling the sun.

insulation Material used to stop heat, electricity or sound from passing through a surface.

internal combustion engine An engine in which the fuel is burned inside the engine, such as in a car or jet.

laser A device that produces an intense beam of light.

lift The force that enables an aircraft to fly. Lift is produced when an aircraft's wings or a helicopter's rotor blades cut through the air.

light Electromagnetic waves that the human eye can detect. Different wavelengths are seen as different colors, with red being the longest and violet the shortest.

liquid crystal display (LCD) The type of display, or screen, used by electronic calculators and digital watches.

maglev A magnetic levitation train that floats above a special track. Magnetic fields support the train's weight and move it along the track.

magnetron The part of a microwave oven and radar equipment that produces microwaves.

microphone A device for changing sound into a varying electrical current.

molecule A group of atoms linked together. Chemical substances are made from molecules.

motor A device for changing electricity into movement, such as the spinning motion of a shaft.

N-type silicon A form of silicon that has been treated so that it contains extra electrons.

objective lens The lens, or group of lenses, which forms the image in a microscope, telescope or a pair of binoculars.

orbit The path of a planet around the sun, or a satellite around the Earth.

oxygen The gas that is essential for life and also for combustion. Oxygen makes up 20 percent of the air around us.

persistence of vision The illusion of movement produced when viewing a film or television. Our eyes see a series of still pictures moving as one.

photodiode A light-sensitive device that varies the size of an electric current flowing through it according to the amount of light that falls on it.

prism A wedge-shaped block of glass used to refract or reflect light.

P-type silicon A form of silicon that has been treated so that it contains fewer electrons.

pulley A wheel with a groove around the rim. A rope can be threaded around the rims of several pulleys to make it easier to lift a heavy weight.

radar A method for locating distant objects, such as aircraft, by sending out bursts of radio waves and detecting any reflections that bounce back.

radiation Energy given out by an object in the form of particles or electromagnetic waves.

radio telescope An instrument designed to detect radio waves from distant parts of the universe.

rocket A vehicle propelled by burning a mixture of fuel and a substance containing oxygen.

rotor The part of a machine that rotates.

satellite An object that orbits a star or planet. Satellites may be natural (moons) or artificial (spacecraft).

shutter The part of a camera that opens for a fraction of a second when you take a picture to let light fall on the film behind it.

silicon A common substance found in sand and clay. It is used in computer chips and solar cells.

software Another word for computer programs, the instructions that make computers work.

solar cell A device that converts sunlight directly into electricity.

stator The part of a rotary machine that does not move.

submarine A large craft that can travel underwater for long distances unaided by any other craft.

submersible A small craft that can dive to great depths underwater. A submersible is much smaller than a submarine, and it is carried to and from its dive location on the deck of a ship.

thrust The force of a jet engine or rocket engine that drives the engine forward.

turbine A machine designed to make a flowing gas or liquid turn a shaft. The gas or liquid hits the angled blades of the turbine and makes them rotate.

turbogenerator An electricity generator driven by a turbine.

ultrasound A high-pitched sound that humans cannot hear.

valve A device used to regulate the flow of a gas or a liquid, or to turn it on and off.

waveguide A hollow tube used to channel microwaves from one place to another.

weight The heaviness of an object, caused by gravity pulling on it.

X-rays Electromagnetic waves that can pass through soft parts of the body. X-rays are used to create images, on photographic film or a computer screen, of the inside of the body.

Stethoscope

Fax machine

SLR camera

Cement truck

Bicycle

Index

Picture Credits

(t=top, b=bottom, l=left, r=right, c=centre, F=front, C=cover, B=back, Bg=background)
Ad-Libitum, 4tl, 7tr, 9tr, 11tr, 14cl, 15br, 15c, 19cr, 20cl, 21tr, 22bl, 23br, 23tr, 24bl, 32tl, 33cr, 35tr, 36bl, 41cr, 42tc (Luna Park Amusements Pty Ltd, Australia), 46b, 46cl, 49tr, 50bl, 50tl, 54tl (Australian National Maritime Museum), 60bct, 60br, 62cl, 62tl, 63br, 63tr (S. Bowey). **Austral International**, 28bl (FPG International). **Australian Picture Library**, 45tr (M. Smith/Retna Pictures), 26/27 (S. Vidler). **Bruce Coleman Ltd**, 6bl (M. Ide/Orion Press). **Heather Angel**, 34cl, 34tcl, 34tl. **The Image Bank**, 31cl (A. Pasieka). **International Photographic Agency**, 37cr, 57br (SuperStock). **Panos Pictures**, 9br (J. Dugast). **The Photo Library, Sydney**, 24tl (C. Bjornberg/Photo Researchers, Inc), 45bl (J. Burgess/SPL), 15tr (M. King), 58tl (NASA/SPL), 27tr (NRAO/SPL), 52l (Photo Researchers, Inc), 54bc (C. Secula), 29tr (SPL). **Photo Researchers, Inc**, 8bl (J. Steinberg). **Robert Harding**

Picture Library, 14tl. **Tezuka Production Co Ltd**, 43br (O. Tezuka). **Tom Stack & Associates**, 13tc (G. Vaughn).

Illustration Credits

Colin Brown/Garden Studio, 18/19c, 18b, 19tr, 19b, 44/45c, 44l, 44br, 63tcr. **Lynette R. Cook**, 5r, 58/59b, 58b, 58tr, 62bcl. **Christer Eriksson**, 4bl, 4c, 4tr, 39–42c (Luna Park Amusements Pty Ltd, Australia). **Rod Ferring**, 50/51c, 51tr. **Chris Lyon/Brihton Illustration**, 14/15c. **Martin Macrae/Folio**, 54/55c, 55br. **David Mathews/Brihton Illustration**, 36/37c, 37br, 63cr (Pentax, CR Kennedy & Co, Australia). **Peter Mennim**, 4/5b, 30l, 30b, 31r. **Darren Pattenden/Garden Studio**, 24/25c, 24tc, 25r, 60bl. **Oliver Rennert**, 6/7c, 7br (Vestas-Danish Wind Technology A/S), 8/9c, 9bc. **Trevor Ruth**, 28/29c. **Stephen Seymour/Bernard Thornton Artists, UK**, 10/11t, 10/11b, 10b, 11b,

52/53c, 52bc, 52tl, 53c. **Nick Shewring/Garden Studio**, 46/47c, 47tr, 47br. **Kevin Stead**, 2/3, 20/21c, 21br, 21c, 38/43c, 63bcr. **Ross Watton/Garden Studio**, 22/23c, 23cr, 48/49c, 48bl, 49bc, 49br, 61bc. **Rod Westblade**, 5tc, 12/13c, 13br, 15bc, 16/17c, 16l, 17br, 26c (Radiotelescope, Parkes, NSW, CSIRO Australia), 26b, 27b, 29br, 31bc, 32/33c, 32bl, 33tr, 42r (Luna Park Amusements Pty Ltd, Australia), 56/57c, 56br, 57bc, 59c, 60/61t, 60/61c, 60bc, 61bl, 61br, 62bl, endpapers, icons. **David Wood**, 1, 34/35c, 34tc, 35br, 62tcl.

Cover Credits

Christer Eriksson, FCc (Luna Park Amusements Pty Ltd, Australia). **David Mathews/Brihton Illustration**, FCcl (Pentax, CR Kennedy & Co, Australia). **Oliver Rennert**, BCtl. **Trevor Ruth**, BCbr. **Stock Photos**, Bg (Phototake). **Rod Westblade**, FCcr.